WE DISSENT

We Dissent

Edited by Hoke Norris

ST MARTIN'S PRESS, NEW YORK

INTRODUCTION

The purpose of this book is to give voice to the opposition in the South. There is an opposition, and it is growing in size, diligence, influence and effectiveness. Not all its members oppose segregation. But they do oppose—they most emphatically dissent from—the rabid segregationists and all their works: The White Citizens Councils, the Ku Klux Klan, the closers of public schools, the wielders of clubs at bus stations, the advocates of interposition and nullification and other legal absurdities invoked in the name of freedom and states' rights.

It is the South's misfortune, however—and the incalculable misfortune of the United States in its daily confrontation of a world predominately colored—that violence and absurdity are often the only Southern symbols that reach the rest of humanity. If our book can inform the rest of the nation, and of the world, of this opposition—this large, growing and most loyal opposition—then it will have served its purpose.

All the writers represented here are Southern-born, Southern-raised, white Protestants. In selecting the contributors to this book about segregation, I practiced that degree of segregation myself. I wanted no fraudulent issue of "outside interference" raised against its contents; I wanted no racial or religious prejudice directed at any of its contributors. I wanted the issues uncluttered and unobscured by any irrelevancy. Our non-Protestant, non-white readers will, I am sure, understand that motivation.

And so, as you read, remember that these are Southerners

talking about themselves and each other. They don't always agree. I didn't expect that they would (and no writer in this book can be held accountable for the opinions and conclusions of any other writer here). Sometimes their judgments of themselves and other Southerners may seem harsh, sometimes too gentle. Whatever your reaction, remember that you are reading the honest, unfettered utterances of the honest, the free and the unafraid.

These Southerners also speak at times about the rest of the nation. To us who have moved North, it often seems that we are now surrounded by a near vacuum occupied only by talk without action. This empty talk issues from self-styled "liberals" willing to die vicariously for the Negro in the South but unmoved to busy themselves on behalf of the Negro in the North. It is easy, and tempting, to be virtuous if your virtue is never tested. It is a challenge of a man's fiber and guts if in being brotherly, and courageous, he risks economic, social or political disadvantage, if not destruction. I admire the writers here who still live in the South and are yet willing to voice their most personal concern over what is happening in and to the South. Those of us who have moved away know the decisions they have had to make, and the integrity with which they confront man as he is and as he ought to be.

Having made their difficult decisions, these writers present an example that might be followed with advantage by people everywhere. Let all Southerners, and all Americans, all human beings, conduct as searching and as honest an appraisal of themselves, their conditions, and their past, present and future. Perhaps then we might hope that some day we will begin emerging from the darkness of prejudice, bigotry, animosity and greed that imperils the future of the nation and the world. For the nation, as for the individual, the unexamined life is not only not worth living; it may in fact be impossible to live it at all much longer.

But there is no quick, easy solution to the problems illuminated by the writers of *We Dissent*. One should regard with firm suspicion any man who argues that there is a single quick, easy, sure cure for humanity's ills—for perplexity, conflict and prejudice, for blindness, ignorance and stupidity. But there are always long, hard cures that can be applied to society, government and the human soul. It is to these cures that the writers of this book direct your attention. There may never be a complete paradise, but toward it we must never cease striving if man is to endure.

Into the hands of stubborn but benign realists I now commit you.

HOKE NORRIS

Summer, 1962

ACKNOWLEDGMENTS

Acknowledgment of the right to reprint material contained herein is made, with appreciation, to the following periodicals and writers:

The Saturday Evening Post and Ralph McGill for "The South Will Change."

The New York Times Magazine and Hodding Carter III for "Meanwhile, in Mississippi—Solidarity Forever?"

The Chicago Sun-Times and Hoke Norris for "Red Roses and Redstones."

Readers interested in further study of the South are advised to seek out books by the authors represented in *We Dissent*. Their books are listed in the biographical notes that precede our 13 articles.

CONTENTS

WE DISSENT

OUR CHANGING SOUTH: A CHALLENGE

Wilma Dykeman & James Stokely . . .

Writers, husband and wife living in Newport, Tenn., co-authors of *Neither Black Nor White* (winner of the Hillman Award in 1957 as the best book of the year on race relations, civil liberties, or world peace) and *Seeds of Southern Change: The Life of Will W. Alexander* (University of Chicago Press, 1962); authors, separately or in collaboration, of articles in many magazines; (Mr. Stokely, a native of Newport, is the member of the family that founded the canning firm, and is an alumnus of the University of Tennessee; Mrs. Stokely, a native of Asheville, graduated at Northwestern University and is the author of *The French Broad*, in the Rivers of America Series, and a novel, *The Tall Woman*, published in the spring of 1962).

Let us begin at the beginning: with the land.

The earliest explorers, the first colonizers, the builders of empire, the hopeful immigrants from debtors' prisons and landlord-ridden farms and religious persecutions, the speculators and adventurers and settlers, and terrified slaves with gleaming black skins—they came to the southern part of the United States and they found an abundant land. There were incredible forests of pine and cypress and hardwoods the likes of which shall not be seen again. Grass grew thick in the meadows, succulent canebrakes were plentiful and, with the mast from the towering forests, provided food for deer and buffalo, bear and wild fowls and all manner of game that fattened on the land.

With a lengthy outer coastline that stretched along an ocean and a gulf, this South had also a vast inner network of rivers and streams. Beneath its soil lay deposits of minerals—coal, clay, petroleum, natural gas, iron, zinc, bauxite, and a variety of others—and above it was a climate more temperate than that of the North or West.

And with this abundance of the land and richness of resources and favorable climate, the settlers and traders and entrepreneurs founded the great single-crop kingdoms. There was tobacco, rice, sugar, and cotton, and none could have come into being or flourished without another factor: the human resources of Africa and the extension of African slavery that followed the opening up of the New World.

Cotton became king of the Southern crops. A fertile crescent, stretching from the southeastern corner of Virginia through eastern North Carolina, cutting a wide swath across South Carolina, Georgia, Alabama, Mississippi, Louisiana, and up into a corner of Texas and Arkansas—this was the heart of the cotton kingdom; it became known as the Black Belt, because of its dark and fertile soil. Slavery, too, was most concentrated here and gave an added meaning to the name.

It was this part of the South, this fertile crescent, this Black Belt, that managed to stamp a single image on the whole wide and varied region. No matter the independent hill dwellers in the mountains of Virginia and Tennessee and Kentucky, the Carolinas and Georgia and Arkansas; no matter the stock raisers and small farmers and merchants in the uplands of Florida, Alabama, Mississippi, and the other states—it was the columned plantation house that became the standard symbol of all the Southern way of life, and it was the cotton boll that became the region's unofficial emblem. The indisputable right of white men to own black men—the strength of their muscles, the allegiances of their minds, the fruits of their labor, and their children—was the credo, not of one area within the region, not of any one group, but of all the South; at least this was the uniform image accepted by outsiders. Within the South there were always Southerners who knew that their way of life, their work and belief, was not part of this stereotype.

Many of them spoke and prayed and debated during the years before Civil War brought the South emancipation from chattel slavery. They protested the moral Christian wrong, the political democratic ambiguity, the personal anguish, of slavery. Some of them started the first weekly newspaper in America dedicated to the abolition of slavery. A few of those who were slaveholders freed their servants because, as one Alabama planter said, slavery was "inconsistent with the Great Truth that all men are created equal." As Professor Charles G. Sellers, Jr., has pointed out, "The key to the tragedy of Southern history is the paradox of the slaveholding South's devotion to liberty."

In more recent years, as the South has moved toward emancipation from the subtler bonds of segregation by race, there have been those who followed the tradition of protest against injustice and affirmation in the challenge of change. For it is most ironic that precisely when the South has resisted all change, she has been required to make the greatest changes.

To maintain the status quo a century ago, a bloody war was fought that shattered forever that status quo and brought deeper dislocations in Southern life than any peaceful read-justments could possibly have wrought. In a blind resistance to any alteration in Southern patterns of behavior, a loud and defiant segment of Southerners in this century, this decade, have shocked the world with their violence, or their apathy in the face of violence. They, too, are discovering that conflict reaps its own whirlwind of change, more devastating than any they could envision.

Change in the South is no longer debatable. It is already a demonstrable fact, reshaping the face of the region, refashioning the life of every person in it. Yet its continuing and over-all presence is still to be admitted. Each new manifestation brings inherent problems and promises. Control of the situation lies in analyzing the problems and diminishing them, while evaluating the promises and bringing them to fullest fruition.

The thorniest problem holds the largest promise in the South today: the entrance of the Negro into the mainstream of the Southern way of life. At the same time, as a congressman from the Deep South, Frank E. Smith, wrote a few years ago, "Willingly or not, and knowingly or not, the South is finally entering the mainstream of American life." As these two movements lend impetus to each other, they move forward, sometimes haltingly, sometimes harmoniously. But they do move. For if much of the South has thus far had the worst of two possible worlds, the false racist superiorities of the nineteenth century and the cheap extractive industries of the twentieth century, it is time we moved on to seize the best of these two worlds, the humanitarian enlightenment of the nineteenth century and a sound industrial economic base in the twentieth century. This can be achieved only by use of our intelligence, our imagination, and our ability, so far remarkably dormant, at self-analysis and objective, long-range appraisal.

As it was the land that shaped our Southern way of life, so it is the use men made of the land that has brought us to our present paradox: from it come our history and our future survival, our prosperity and our poverty, our enormous problems and our great potential. It was not slavery—or later, segregation—that defined a Southern way of life; too many Southern people never held slaves; too many have doubted the system of segregation. But Southerners, longer and later than any others in our country, have remained close to the land. This has complicated our entrance into the industrial age. Perhaps it has also permitted us certain gifts and understandings that can be of value if we will but use them on the world scene today, as agrarian countries achieve twentieth-century freedom and seek to participate in the prosperity of industrial, scientific discovery.

Thus, with roots firmly planted in the Southern earth—not that of the Black Belt, but upland mountain ground where rocks are so plentiful the land has to be stout to hold them all up—having knowledge unconsciously absorbed in childhood or painfully acquired through experience and contemplation, we dissent.

We dissent from all that is unjust or unworthy (and so widely publicized) in our South today.

We dissent from those myths that have gained currency throughout the region and helped paralyze us in a time calling for action, helped make us numb at a moment when we have need of every sensitive nerve in our human being to bring us through a time of moral and physical crisis.

There is the myth of silence.

This is the myth designed to quell disagreement with a majority—or a vocal and often ruthless minority. It labels Southerners who wish to discuss their racial situation as "trouble-makers," disturbers of the peace at pleasant dinner parties and church socials and club gatherings. This, of course, is somewhat like saying that the diagnostician who pronounces his patient ill of cancer is a trouble-maker.

An outstanding Southern author wrote of her experiences with this silence.

> During the first ten years of my life there were a thousand lynch-ings in the South. It was in this atmosphere of terror and brutality, of internal and external disorder, that we were taught our lessons in segregation. No wonder so many Southerners of my age cling to it. We were told as children never to question it, never to talk about it. This silence which is today so puzzling to others is a built-in silence; its foundations go down to babyhood, to our mother's hushed whis-pering; there is a hypnotic quality about such learning and only the rebellious mind, the critical intelligence or the loving heart can hope to defy it.

What we have to fear in the South, and the world, today is not dispute—but silence. In the twilight of nondiscussion, minds do not grow tough; they do not even grow. In a poem called "Stronger Lessons" Walt Whitman asked, "Have you learned lessons only of those who admired you, and were tender with you, and stood aside for you? Have you not learned great lessons from those who reject you, and brace themselves against you, or who treat you with contempt, or dispute the passage with you?"

Then there is the myth that we can have universal education of our citizens without universal participation in the full rights of citizenship.

After 1877, the end of Reconstruction, the South preserved the principle of public education but insured, through law, that it would remain segregated. Perhaps the remarkable point, however, is that education for Negroes was accepted by the white South as a necessary commitment. That commitment sowed the seed for today's ferment as surely as an acorn grows into an oak.

When the white South accepted the principle of public education for the Negro and then surrounded it with walls of segregation, it tried to perpetuate a paradox doomed to eventual failure. The paradox was inherent in an attempt to promote that very thing whose essence is change (education) while surrounding it with a code designed to insure the *status quo* (segregation). When the South set its course along the path of education, no matter how scanty, no matter how unequal, for all its people, it started the journey that led inevitably to the 1954 Supreme Court decision outlawing segregation by race in the public schools. We are seeing blasted today the myth that people can be fully committed to education in a democracy without also being committed to every person's mobility on the social, political, and professional ladder.

The myth of our aristocracy has persisted.

We have too often bemused ourselves into believing in a leadership of aristocracy in the South when in reality we were relinquishing the reins to demagogues and knaves. A Southern professor of English has made an excellent observation on this point.

The South is rightfully proud of its aristocratic heritage, but all too often we forget that aristocracy is a state of mind, a morality, the conditions of which are sacrifice and obligation and a concern for the welfare of others. The aristocratic mind is the mind least of all afraid of losing its place in society. That fear belongs to bourgeois morality, by which I mean that morality which views life in terms of rights rather than obligations, and difficult as we find it to admit, Southern behavior surrounding the Negro question has been inescapably bourgeois. If this morality is allowed to maintain its control over the South, the South is doomed.

Too frequently, during the past years, we have yielded our truly aristocratic traditions to a leadership of opportunism. Men in bedsheets have become a popular symbol of the South, rather than men in the caps and gowns of scholarly learning. Men with emotional appeals to stampede the fears of the multitude have out-shouted those who would reason and lead the hopes of the people. But not always. Not forever. Here and there the myth cracks. The aristocracy of enlightened concern and obligation to society—an aristocracy open to all —revives and will move again in the South.

There is the myth of the outsider.

Purveyors of this myth contend that the ferment for equal rights and opportunities would not have arisen in the South except for "outside agitators." Now resentment against strangers participating in what are considered to be local affairs has always been strong in the South. During the Civil War, Zeb Vance, that Governor of North Carolina who jealously guarded his state's independence against all encroachments, from Confederacy and Union alike, called some of the Virginians who had been put in command of North Carolina troops "outsiders." And the label was used with not a little bitterness.

The efforts of some white Southerners today to convince themselves that Negro aspirations are being stirred by foreign agitation or alien philosophy are only self-deceptive, however. The South cannot come to logical grips with its racial situation until it realizes that it is not the outer prompting of Communism but the inner functioning of democracy that keeps our nation, and our region, in process of change. Indeed, by his very struggle for equality the Negro is seeking, not alienation from democracy, but greater participation in it. It is the sharpest irony that some of our political demagogues accuse Negroes of being inspired by totalitarian agitators to enjoy the fullness of democracy. We cannot give the Communist Manifesto credit for arousing those dreams and actions which are the very heart and guts of our Declaration of Independence and American Constitution. There was also an inspiring non-Russian document called the Emancipation Proclamation. And the roots of all these might be traced to the Sermon on the Mount.

Last, and by no means least, there is the myth, largely unstated but demonstrated in many of our attitudes and acts, that our Southern experience is part of the past but not of the future. This is true only if we make it so.

Of course, the South has a past, and remembrance of that past, and allegiance to it. Part of our problem and opportunity today is how to preserve the best of that past—the sane realism of such Southerners as Washington, Jefferson, Mason, Madison, Monroe, Wilson—to insure a richer present and a surer future. And this is true not only of the South but of a large part of the world's new nations. Therein lies our unique opportunity.

One of the dilemmas facing every emergent nation in Asia and Africa, and even the old nations entering a world of new space horizons, is this synthesis of tradition and innovation. We stand midway between our grandfathers and our grand-children, and we bear a responsibility to each. We must discharge it with resourcefulness and justness.

It is imperative for Southerners to remember that our minority is the world's majority. The fate of all of us in the Atlantic community of the white world—16 per cent of the world's peoples consuming 70 per cent of the world's wealth

—is inextricably linked to the fate of those colored billions consuming only 30 per cent of the world's wealth. It has been pointed out frequently that our treatment of the Negro in the South may reflect the treatment we, in turn, shall expect abroad. It is time for us to examine this truism more closely and clarify a very important point for the other countries on our globe.

The violence that has erupted in parts of the South over Negro-white relationships, that violence with which we dissent most sharply, is *not* due to an undemocratic and static society. It arises from our very participation in a democratic and changing society. No sane person would contend that we have reached perfection here in the United States, but neither would any concerned citizen argue that we have given up struggling toward it. It is this struggle that finds most acute form in the South today. It is this very conviction, that America and the South are not frozen societies forever fixed in their present molds, that makes Negroes demand payment on promissory notes of equality issued long ago, that makes white citizens re-examine the social arrangements by which they live.

We are part of a world-wide experience, for we are undergoing a revolution in the South, economic, social, cultural, spiritual, and no revolution ever took place without a struggle. To borrow a familiar phrase, then, the winds of change are not only blowing across the world, they are ruffling the South. The change is here, not only inevitable but irrevocable. What is not and never has been inevitable is the price we pay for change: the price in bitterness, in violence, in weakened institutions, in distorted traditions. We can see change as an unwanted harvest to be trampled in the fields, or as a seedbed to be cultivated for future nourishment.

Thus, implicit in our dissent is also a larger, more important, assent. We believe that the South long ago captured the past and made of it a unique heritage; we believe that the South can also capture the future and make to it a unique contribution.

The land, turning green again where foresight has planted new forests and new grass across the South, the coastline along the Atlantic and the Gulf, an abundance of water inland, minerals and a wide range of climate, all these are still assets, gifts if you please, of the region. But it is its people who will thrust the South forward into leadership for tomorrow, or hold it back in bondage to yesterday.

There is excitement in living and working and growing in the South today, for it is the challenge of the twentieth century in all parts of the present world that now faces the Southerner. The challenge is to confront boldly and realistically the question of how the Southern way may be merged with the American way without becoming submerged. Released from the confinement of an overriding concern with race and the costly toll of segregation, the best meaning of the Southern tradition could bring a new balance to American life: balance between the urban and the rural, between man and the machine, between making a living and making a life.

It is the nature of this challenge that must be brought home to Southerners today. The choice lies between being overwhelmed in the inevitable tide of equality and freedom which is moving humanity everywhere, or seizing that tide and using it to capture the imagination and allegiance of the world. We deny that there is anywhere a monolithic South that will not realize the dimensions of this choice—its magnitude and meaning—and move to meet it with courage and honor.

THE SOUTH WILL CHANGE

Ralph McGill . . .

Publisher of the *Atlanta Constitution*, syndicated columnist and author; native of Soddy, Tenn., attended Vanderbilt University
and the University of Miami; U.S. Marines, 1918-19; reporter and
sports editor, *The Banner*, Nashville, 1922-23; sports editor of *The
Constitution* 1931-33, executive editor 1938-42, editor 1942-1960;
member of the board, Fund for the Advancement of Education;
awarded Rosewald fellowship, 1937-38, for travel in Europe; Pulitzer
prize for editorial writing, 1958; member of the Georgia Academy of
Social Sciences; author of *Israel Revisited; Church, a School;* and *The
Fleas Come with the Dog.* (Mr. McGill recently won the Atlantic
Monthly magazine's $5,000 non-fiction prize for his book *The South
and the Southerner*, which Atlantic-Little, Brown will publish in
the spring of 1963).

In the long years of the Negro's discouragingly slow advance
against his country's long-entrenched practices of segregation,
the historically unique feature of this struggle has been largely
unnoted. It is that the Negro, a distinct racial minority, was
trying to become more American—not less. He was not, like
some of the minorities of Europe, seeking to be set apart, to be

recognized as a separate race with special privileges and status. He had already experienced being excluded from the national life, and he did not like it. He wanted to be accepted as a citizen, which the Constitution said he was, and to have the privileges accorded other citizens—no more, no less.

Nor was this all the story. Despite rejections and exploitations, often cunning, cruel, and ruthless, the Negro stubbornly identified himself with America and its promise. He persisted in this, even though his denials often have been stupid and stultifying in coarseness and violence.

When the wars came in 1898, 1917, 1941, and later in Korea, he served as he was permitted. It was experiences of the Korean conflict that precipitated decision to integrate military services. Morale in the segregated units understandably was low. The all-Negro companies became an embarrassment as we emphasized our principles of democracy in the bloody campaign to stop Communist aggression. Jim Crow was cawing raucously and mockingly all the while.

At the conclusion of the Korean armistice, there were twenty-one American G.I.'s who refused exchange and announced they were indorsing Communism and going to Red China. Only three were Negroes. Studies of the twenty-one who stayed revealed some with backgrounds of inadequacies and educational lacks. Yet none of the white soldiers had case histories of discrimination and psychological pressures to match that of the average Negro G.I. It also is true that, despite a consistent campaign by the Communist Party to convince the Negro that Marxism is his most logical political faith, the percentage of Negroes so persuaded is smaller than that of white Americans who have embraced it.

In the face of the whole record it is ironic that the canons of conformity are so fixed, so sicklied o'er with the pale cast of myth and the hypocrisy and falsehood of a separate but equal status, that the Negro's effort to become more American is attacked by extremist opposition as an un-American, Communist plot.

Until very recent years the Negro's total identity was with America. But once African ambassadors began to be heard in the United Nations and political leaders of the new nations began to appear in world conferences, a great many Negroes, especially the more aggressively committed students, began to feel an identification with Africa and its emerging nationalisms. This was, in a sense, healthy. It can become dangerous only if the white-supremacy extremists are permitted to filibuster legitimate civil-rights bills in the Congress and if the states continue to deny the simple uncomplicated rights of equal citizenship.

The familiar rationalizations against doing what is, after all, a necessary and decent thing required by—in addition to the Constitution—the ethics of Judaism, Christianity, and Western civilization long ago lost whatever dubious relevance they may have had. Yet they continue to be repeated by those whose emotional involvement prevents perspective. These irrelevancies are the essential ingredient of the White Citizens Councils' speeches and printed propaganda.

After the 1954 school decision, for example, one began to read statements by leaders of massive-defiance groups to the effect that "To admit Negro children to school would pull down the level of classroom performance. They aren't ready for it yet."

Now the irony of this rationalization was that it was, with some notable exceptions, true. What the rationalists did not realize they were doing was indicting the system of segregated education. It had been separate. It had never been equal. It had been callously, heartlessly maintained in a most unequal manner. The white schools of the South were much inferior to the national averages, but they were far better than those for Negroes. The major inequities are familiar. The amount spent per Negro student was substantially less than that per white student. Later years have seen most urban pay scales equalized, but not all are, and for many years Negro teachers have suffered serious discrimination in salaries.

In myriad other ways Negro children in the South were deprived of opportunity to participate in the race of life.

In a number of Southern states, as late as 1957, sums as low as two dollars or three dollars per pupil were being spent for libraries for white pupils while a few cents or nothing at all was being spent for Negro children.

For years after the development of school-bus transportation, 70 or 80 per cent of the white children of the Deep South states requiring such service were provided it. But in some states not more than 10 per cent of the Negro children were so served.

It was a common practice in a number of Southern states to supply Negro schools with used or outdated textbooks discarded by white students. Negro schools were more crowded and had more double sessions. Vocational training was rarely first class for either race.

Advanced training in medicine, dentistry, law, nursing, architecture, electrical, mechanical, and textile engineering in Southern state institutions was open to Negro students only after court decisions began to crack a few doors.

Southern politicians and a dismaying number of businessmen have been heard to say that the Negro can't learn, that he is inherently incapable of achievement. For this to be said, in the face of the educational discrimination that historically has existed, reveals either an unworthy ignorance of the facts or a deliberate distortion of them.

School superintendents, psychologists, truancy supervisors, and juvenile-court officers in the Eastern and Western states know the lacks of both white and Negro children who have come out of the average Southern school—especially those of rural areas. The level of work in many classrooms has been reduced. Desegregated schools are faced with the need to create remedial classes and to screen newcomers carefully to determine the grade for which they are prepared.

This background helps explain other things too—all very well known to sociologists and social caseworkers.

The Negro children who had no access to libraries, whose classroom instruction was poor, who had little home incentive to go to school, who had to walk long distances, who had little or no access to vocational skills are the Negro adults of today —thousands of them in big-city slums, struggling in marginal jobs, or picking up what work they can find in unskilled capacities. And always there are the white products of the same system, the cruel cost of which, in human and dollar loss, daily becomes more apparent.

There is another rationalization that is an inevitable feature of the talks and writings of the prosegregationist politicians and apologists. It runs like this: "Let the Negro show some responsibility of citizenship before he is given the ballot. Let him prove himself ready to assume some of the burdens of civic life."

That this sort of nonsense should be written and spoken in heat and anger and received with applause by Klan-type mentalities is fantastic. It is even more preposterous than the arguments that the Negro is not capable of learning. After all, there were some schools. More often than not they were a disgrace to the flag that flew over them, but there were schools. But, in voting, there are to this day many rural areas where no Negro votes at all. There are others where a few are registered. And there are cities in at least four southern states where the most-qualified Negro finds it extremely difficult to be registered. The depths of this deprivation lend eloquence to statistics. As late as midsummer of 1961 only 25 per cent of the Negroes in the Southern states who had reached voting age were registered to vote.

During the summer of 1961, for example, civil-rights cases were filed by the United States Department of Justice in Clarke and Forrest counties, Mississippi. Clarke County, in the east-central area, had more than 50 per cent of her white citizens registered. A disputed total of not more than six of the 2988 eligible Negroes was on the registration books. In Forrest County, in southeast Mississippi, about half the 22,431 eligible whites were registered. Only twenty-five of the 7495 Negroes had been able to become qualified. There was, in the Justice Department files, a long record of attempted registrations that failed.

In filing suit Attorney General Robert Kennedy said, "Negroes in those two counties still are being deprived of the right to vote, the fundamental right of all American citizens. It is our responsibility under law to guarantee this right, and we will meet the responsibility . . ."

The reply of Mississippi's Gov. Ross Barnett will almost certainly be at least a footnote in the history of the time. "I don't understand why they want to interfere with local self-government," he said. "Local government is the thing that has made this country great."

It is not comforting to know that there are those who feel so alien to the United States and its principles that the fundamental rights of citizens have so little meaning.

This inability to vote has inevitable side effects. The Negro in the South has not been permitted to participate in community discussions about the problems of schools or of other civic affairs. It is only in the last few years that an occasional Negro has been elected to a school board in some of the larger cities.

Not only was the Negro barred from any opportunity to gain understanding of local government; he had to listen in public and on radio and television to demagogic speakers who tried to outdo one another in their pledges to keep the Nigger (or Nigra) in his place. Nor was this all. The Negro was confronted daily with a picture of government which plainly and officially, through state statutes and municipal ordinances, gave him an inferior position as a human being. It was not logical to expect him to acquire any competence or interest in civic responsibilities. Yet there are Southerners today who, in the face of the record, say that the Negro isn't ready to participate in government. Let him earn the right "by demonstrating his responsibility as a citizen," they say.

That all of this is a costly piece of business to us as a country is plain. The South will pay the heaviest price. But in these days when population is used to mobility, an illiterate, untrained white or Negro boy or girl from Alabama or Georgia can quickly become a hoodlum in Illinois or California, a social-welfare statistic in Philadelphia or Milwaukee. A national responsibility for an end to discriminations in the rights of citizens and for equitable public education is inescapable. We already have a problem of two generations, adult and young, which have filled the slums of our industrial cities.

Another oft-repeated argument against citizenship rights for the Negro is based on irrational intermarriage fears, stemming from God knows what Freudian experiences and guilts. This is a real puzzler.

Do those who use the argument mean to imply that, of the 180,000,000 Americans, only Southerners need segregation laws to protect them from such marriages? Questions like this bring only recriminations, some vile and violent, never a logical discussion.

A question automatically poses itself when morality, law, and economics begin to make themselves felt.

What are our chances of avoiding a continuance of irrational processes? The answer is that the chances are good. There will be much resistance to desegregation and some of it will be violent. But there are new conditions. We are not, to be honest, having too much success changing the hearts and minds of men, as President Eisenhower suggested be done to solve the problem. But we are moving. Attorney General Kennedy saved the lives of perhaps a hundred or more persons by dispatching U.S. marshals to Montgomery, Alabama, where a Federal judge, native of the state, later severely reprimanded the police department for its failure to be on hand in enough numbers to cope with the mob during the Freedom Rider troubles. The Attorney General also made it plain that no community may support its own peculiar customs by attempts to maim or kill other citizens. The people of Alabama already are beginning to be grateful to the attorney general for saving their state from an even more shocking excess in lawlessness. In time they may thank him publicly.

There are no evidences of wholesale integration, but this has not been the objective. Negro leadership has sought to make the Negro a citizen in the full sense of the word. Whatever integration takes place in the private sectors of life is for persons privately to determine. But if we begin with a date as late as May, 1954, when the school decision was published, we can see how vast has been the change in the legal status of the Negro.

Laws and courts have declared and defined the Negro's equal citizenship.

What the nation is just beginning to understand is that the Negro's efforts at citizenship now are being officially opposed only by those who are defying law, or clinging to contradictory state laws which have been declared unconstitutional.

That desegregation will for some time be a process confined largely to the urban complexes of the South, and the nation, is plain. The rural areas have not yet been affected directly, although all feel the heat of change. But these eddies of semi-feudal ruralism are dying. Their people are leaving to go to the cities—where resolvement will be had.

The businessmen of most Southern cities now understand that they cannot have lawlessness, violence, and closed or crippled schools—and progress. They already are looking with questioning eyes at the blatant White Citizens Councils' leadership and at the bull-like antics of police staffs which have been party to violence.

So, as we move forward in history, it can be said that the status of desegregation now is at the point where all who oppose it are in defiance or technical evasion of law. And room for evasive maneuver is about used up.

A lot of persons, mostly in trade, are not really concerned with the principles involved. But they are increasingly interested in a climate of law and order in which business and community life may flourish.

But while this force is most influential, it cannot be said that the moral influence is absent. All Southerners, save the most obtuse and insensitive, have long carried a private weight of guilt about the inequities of segregation. This weight now tilts many over to the side of justice and humanity.

Prejudice, bigotry, and defiance remain. But this is still a nation which understands it must live by law. It is no longer lawful to deprive any citizen of his rights to vote and to attend the public schools, parks, auditoriums, and concerts. The sit-ins and the Freedom Riders spotlighted economic injustice.

The excitement and challenge of the Negro's determined drive to become more American increasingly outweigh the forces which seek to influence him to abandon his identity as an American. The Black Muslims represent a religion alien to the American traditions. Chrisitanity and the Bible have more appeal than Mohammed and the Koran. In addition, the Muslims propose a number of ghetto states. Only the most despairing and neurotic are likely to be attracted by such principles. Nor is there any sign that Communism is becoming more persuasive.

Dr. Martin Luther King, the student sit-in leaders, the Freedom Riders, the intelligent and able leaders of the N.A.A.C.P., the Urban League, and other organizations joined in common cause might well be called the abolitionist force of the present. They are giving the South and the nation a new image of the Negro. And, perhaps even more important, they have made it possible for the Southern Negro to change his own image. In time the South, which has been deceived by its local political leadership into damning and fearing the N.A.A.C.P. and Martin Luther King, will come to appreciate the beneficial Americanism of this leadership. They will come to see, as some already do, that Doctor King and the N.A.A.C.P. acted always from a basis of law, not violence or defiance of law.

WE DISSENT : 24

This could not be said of all the White Citizens Councils, the Klans, and the zoolike lesser organizations that sprang up to incite lawlessness. Had the Negro leadership also used violence, instead of passive resistance and the processes of law, the results would have been dreadful.

Nothing in the South is left unchanged by the changes that are occurring. And for the overwhelming majority of Negroes there is a pioneering determination to become more American, not less. The Negro also will always be a part of the South. Millions feel themselves Southerners as well as Americans. And as growing numbers of white Southerners learn to appreciate the new image of the Negro as a citizen, the South will accept him as such.

Day-by-day opposition to the Negro's rights to equal citizenship finds itself more and more in the position of opposing the law and the Constitution. Tactics of delay and defiance cannot long sustain themselves, particularly in the urban communities, where the total of qualified Negro voters grows larger and larger. The depressed rural defiance will, in good time, fall of its own weight. The end is not yet in sight—but it is there.

OUR ROAD TO DAMASCUS

Kathleen Keen Sinnett . . .

Native of Memphis, Tenn., lived in Mississippi and Arkansas; bachelor's and master's degree at University of Mississippi; doctor's degree from Radcliffe in clinical psychology, 1957; formerly on clinical staff of Menninger Foundation; now teaching psychology and sociology at Washburn University, Topeka, Kan.

Every society and religion, ancient or modern, has enshrined a "golden rule" as the principal guide of conduct for men's lives. In its essence, this rule declares another's humanity to be like my own and entitled to the same respect. Most societies have added codicils and modifiers of some kind to this general rule so as to permit, foster, or enforce certain exclusions and exceptions. But these codicils are held uneasily; the boundaries of inclusion and exclusion waver in the inner conflicts that always arise when men attempt to live out contradictions.

The white Southerner has violated this principle basically in his usurpation of the right to tell another person *where* he can eat, sleep, walk, drink, sit, reside. (The denial of the vote to Negroes is required, of course, to assure they have no voice at all in their own fate.) The issue is not whether the Negro eats at the same kind of table or studies in the same kind of classroom; it is in the right of each individual under the law to determine these matters for himself, or, if regulation is involved, to have the same regulations applied impartially to every person. This is the basic civil right, an inalienable human right, which the white South has appropriated and now sits hunched over, refusing to give back, like a dog with a bone it has stolen.

But every Southerner knows how this bone was stolen, and feels at least an occasional mild uneasiness about segregation. I believe that every Southerner *without exception* has experienced some distress on this account. But some of them cannot face the psychic burdens of admitting this distress partially or temporarily, or even secretly to themselves. As many social scientists have suggested, these keepers of shameful secrets may be the men who create turmoil in the South. They violently oppose all social change because they secretly fear the total collapse of an unstable inner world. An experience like Paul's on the road to Damascus is probably required to "convert" such persons. Persuasion can accomplish little or nothing. These are the hard-core segregationists who would literally give up every human good, every other ideal they possess, in order to preserve this one. These, then, are the fanatics, and there are not very many of them, but in recent years they have become our most conspicuous Southerners.

Most Southerners can admit, if not to Northerners, then at least to each other, that some conditions of Negro life in the South are or have been undesirable. Many, at times, are able to question the whole system; some have private reservations about particular parts of it; most cannot admit that they would condone methods of terror to enforce it. And even though they may feel that they sincerely believe segregation is the best way of life, they are not prepared to sacrifice every hu-

man good to its preservation. Such people form the vast majority of those residing in the South. I call them the "moderate"
group, not because they take a middle view of segregation, but
because they are reasonable, sensible people who want mainly
the opportunity to live peaceful lives and to bring up their
children at least partly in the traditions taught them by their
own parents.

In the current struggle, these "Southern moderates" have
not yet been very actively involved. Just now, they are the
only persons or groups in the South who can imagine—though
mistakenly—that they still have something to conserve by not
actively taking sides. Southern liberals who have declared
themselves have already lost or have become ready to lose
whatever they have that others could take away. As a group,
the Negroes have nothing to lose but oppression and misery,
and can only gain in self-esteem and dignity through whatever actions they take. No matter how much immediate personal loss a few individual Negroes may suffer, whatever
protests they now make serve the group well. But the ardent
segregationists have everything to lose. Power, status, and
prestige are starting to flow down the drain, and they are busy
holding their fingers over the outlet, clutching with the other
hand for anything that might plug up the leaks.

The silent moderate, numerically a majority, most often
stifles whatever protest he feels, but sometimes expresses it
when he can be sure that what he says won't get himself or
anybody else into trouble. It's usually acceptable to say that
people shouldn't be dragged out of jail and lynched. But
usually the moderate simply conforms in action to the Southern raceways as he has always done, while nourishing his
careful private feelings that he is different from and superior
to the Ku Klux Klan. There are many shades and stripes of

Southern Moderate opinion but four elements of the pattern may be easily identified:

1. The Southern Moderate feels that he is morally superior to those who lynch.
2. He keeps silent.
3. He maintains the traditional Southern racial etiquette both in his personal relations with Negroes and in his public behavior; he conforms without thought to all the ordinary practices of segregation.
4. He is not ready to sacrifice every human good to the preservation of a segregated society in the South.

In short, the moderate Southerner, like the majority of people everywhere, is just a bit of a coward. He wants to stay out of trouble, to tend his shop and cultivate his garden in peace, and he doesn't want to be either a social crusader or a martyr. On the whole, he may be a pretty good guy, but he's nobody's best hope for social revolution of even the most peaceful sort, let alone the kind of dirty bloody struggle this desegregation business often is.

And this moderate-minded man has no idea how hard it would be to break his silence or change his actions, even if the times were not so turbulent or the pressures for conformity were not so insistent. He may also be far *less* tolerant, and far more accepting of the barbaric elements of Southern life, than he or anyone else has realized, because with every action of his social being he lives in and daily supports a system that absolutely requires occasional lynchings of one sort or another in order to perpetuate itself. If there were no Ku Klux Klan, it would be necessary for the moderates to invent one. Only terror has held human beings in the abject subjugation that is the common lot of Negroes in the deep South, a subjugation that is the foundation stone of the *status quo* so dear to the moderate heart. Terror, like any other intense emotion, diminishes after a time; occasional demonstrations are necessary to recreate and maintain it.

So long as the moderate majority can continue going about its daily business in its customary style, segregation is as effectively maintained as the patterns of any stable society. Only the actions of so-called "extremist" groups that imperil the peace and threaten or disrupt the continuity of business-as-usual have brought any significant social change to the deep South. The moderate-minded man as well as the ardent segregationist can, most of the time, continue believing that if "they" would "just let us alone down here," everything would be "all right."

But to speak of "the North" or of "extremist groups" *forcing* desegregation upon a reluctant South is a distorting over-simplification. The real force is the vast and impersonal power of twentieth-century history. The North is compelled by this power to play the role of destiny's agent, sometimes reluctantly and with little conviction. Let us examine very briefly some of the insistent pressures that make up this irresistible force.

The traditional values of the paternalistic, agrarian old South are increasingly ineffective in meeting the needs of the new South's emerging urban-industrial society. So far, the deepest South has repudiated what it considers the impersonal, cash-conscious ways of the industrialized communities, though in so doing it has had nothing to cling to except the fast-fading legend of a Lost Cause that is already a subject either of humor or of bitter scorn to the rest of the world. Segregation, the keystone of the Southern social arch, has taken on increased significance in the conflicts that arise during the transition from agrarian to industrial life. But segregation is only one among many of the Southern traditions menaced by the demands of an urban-industrial community that needs so much talent and skill that it cannot afford the human waste inherent in caste systems. Southern businessmen eager to "attract industry" are usually unaware of the inevitable consequences. Even with such awareness, however, the increasing industrial expansion of the United States could not have been halted at the Mason-Dixon line and the South would not have been willing to renounce prosperity. Thus the South's entry into the social commotion of the Industrial Revolution seems an inevitability.

Social upheaval has everywhere accompanied the Industrial Revolution; it has penetrated a diversity of cultures, and its aftermath has been remarkably consistent. Every heavily industrialized urban center conforms more or less perfectly to this philosophy: If you can produce, you are accepted, and money establishes your social position.

It is hard to imagine any ideals less compatible than these with the social reality of the South during most of the past hundred years. "Good" family connections and the cultured use of an ample leisure time have long counted far more heavily toward high social standing than a sizable income or long hours of hard work. The genteel poverty of the "best" families as pictured in many a Southern novel was a fact of life in the South over many years.

And always Southern society has divided the two races, automatically setting one half of itself above the other. Segregation was an arrangement actually worked out toward the end of the Reconstruction Period as a simple and direct substitution for slavery, but it is now called the "traditional" way. White society can therefore consider it unnecessary to recognize any social differentiations or pretensions to higher status within the subordinated Negro group. Segregation also gave lower-class whites an illusory feeling of superiority that kept them, if not content, at least relatively quiescent under wretched living conditions. Thus it has often been possible for a numerically small group of "Southern aristocrats" to retain firm control of the society. If ever, by some mischance, power slipped from these established factions, at least it didn't slip far. It always fell safely into other white hands, and presently a bargain could be struck. The *status quo* was always restored. No one can expect this very powerful minority to welcome change that results in an equal distribution of political power, but at one time the opposition looked less formidable than it does today.

In the summer of 1954, when I traveled widely in Mississippi, I heard everywhere much puzzled talk about the Supreme Court decision. Over and over I heard such statements as this: "It's a terrible thing, but it's coming and I guess we'll have to get used to it." In the summer of 1960, when I again traveled through the South, I heard much *less* but far more tense and bitter talk about desegregation. This time I heard, "They'll never make us do it—they can't make us do it—we'll show them."

The North, Southern ex-patriates like myself, the Congress, and the Federal Government must be held largely responsible for this change of attitude. By failing to support unequivocally the Supreme Court decision, by failing time and time again to stop, punish, or even censure those who subverted the first scattered and tentative efforts to comply with the demand of the Court, by failing to throw the combined weight of our prestige, influence, and personal effort behind this unprecedented demand for revolutionary change, we have encouraged the growth of an obdurate spirit. Like the balky child

of timid and uncertain parents, the white South now has dug
her heels into the ground, screams "No!" and will not be
budged. Only among Southern Negroes has the Supreme
Court decision of 1954 retained its compelling quality, though
for some of these Negro groups it may seem more and more
like a neglected, fading promise.

But the North, as the agent of destiny, can bring about far
more effective pressures than can the Negroes of the South,
though thus far it has not begun to exert the pressures available
to it. Eight years later, the Federal Government continues to
award defense contracts to Southern industries practicing
segregation or having discriminatory hiring policies; it still
allows segregation in hospital and public health buildings
heavily financed with Federal funds; and two presidents in a
row, of differing political parties, spend time and money in
Southern states with no visible concern for the fact that they
are thereby supporting a social order that is constantly sub-
verting the Constitution they swore to uphold. And I daresay
neither of these two gentlemen has heard much protest from
any of their liberal supporters.

But despite Federal inaction and inconsistency, the old
status quo in the South is steadily dissolving. Unless the moderates begin soon to participate in the forming of a new *status
quo*, the emerging social order will inevitably be shaped by
forces hostile to most aspects of Southern culture, including
many traditions not absolutely incompatible with the temper
of the times. The last chance to preserve any parts of the old
Southern system is for Southern minds to help in the creation
of a new Southern system.

You will recall the treatment accorded the first Freedom
Riders in Alabama and Mississippi. If such incidents became
more intense or more frequent, the deep South would prob-

ably lose either permanently or temporarily a great deal of her political control and autonomy. In this age of instant mass communication, the beating and killing of Negroes can no longer be concealed from an increasingly concerned and ever-growing public. Despite the harassed (and faintly craven?) plea of the attorney general for a "cooling-off period," we cannot avoid segregation-testing action from fear of "inciting to riot." This fear invites the threat of riot as a kind of regional blackmail perpetually opposing all efforts toward desegregation. No nation guided by the rule of law can permit the fear of mob violence to dictate its policy. The speedier an end is made by the Southern public itself to any sort of violent reprisals, the more is the likelihood that the South will be able to retain intact its political autonomy during the period of transition to full integration. The more massive the South's resistance, the more violent and disorderly its action, the more forceful must be the intervention of the Federal Government.

Many integrationists think of segregation simply as the degrading assignment of an inferior position to the Negro race, and are in essence concerned with "rescuing" the Negro from his low position. The extent to which the segregation system deforms the characters and minds of *both* races is not generally appreciated by the public, and of course is hotly denied by the dedicated traditionalists who believe all distinctively Southern traits of mind to be symptoms of superiority. The Southern system requires that its advocate somehow maintain logically opposing beliefs (in the brotherhood of men under God and in the inferiority of Negroes to whites), that he overlook that which is obvious to the most casual observation (that Negroes don't like being segregated and humiliated), and that he perpetually deny the most elemental human reality (the similarity of all other human beings to ourselves). These requirements force mental deformities of great proportion, create minds that must avoid turning inward or probing deeply into any matter, and shape personalities that live only upon polite and banal surfaces, profoundly alienated from the spontaneous emotional life. On the other hand, it is not really remarkable that this century has produced many Southern novelists and writers. Any reflective mind in the Southern environment is so inexorably forced back within itself that its thought must find expression in writing or die. If the social conditions of any region force every intelligent and thoughtful person early in life to resort to secret scribbling, a few good writers are bound to emerge. They may or may not try to break the bonds of caste, but there they are, scribbling away.

Anyone interested in undertaking caste-busting in the near future should be forewarned that it isn't easy for either whites or Negroes to give up the old ways even if they wish to. It is probably much harder now than when I was young, for then there was no particular tension between the races; even so, it was hard enough in the 1940's to escape the traditional patterns.

As far back in my life as I can remember, I have thought Negroes were badly treated in the South and that this was a wrong that should be corrected. For at least the last fifteen years, I have had a deep and continually increasing conviction that any form of segregation is evil, its practice morally shameful to any person, and its effects degrading to all members of both races.

My *attitudes* were all shaped and molded within the South, from the crosscurrents and contradictions that have always existed there. These counterforces, intrinsic to the Southern order, have always produced and always will produce some liberal minds distinctively Southern in outlook. My Southern heritage, however, contributed little toward the *actions* in which I now engage, such as sharing public facilities of all kinds with Negroes, teaching Negro students in the same class-room with whites, having Negro colleagues and friends with whom I am free to discuss or not to discuss the mysteries of racial feeling. These capacities for action I acquired largely in the North where the ways of other persons about me sup-ported my own attempts to act without discrimination. In the Northern environment I could pass for a champion of equality, a paragon of liberal virtue. Yet, in the summer of 1960, the last time I was in the South, I used the white water fountains, the white rest rooms, the white motels, and with my Southern hosts politely refrained from discussing the race question. (In Southern drawing rooms for some time now, it's been in far worse taste to discuss race than to speak of sex.) So, in the South, in the summer of 1960, you could not have distin-guished my routine behavior from that of the most rabid segregationist.

When I was younger, and before I had ever left the South, I tried to break through some of the caste etiquette on a few occasions, to give expression in action to the liberal beliefs that had become important to me. It is still painful to recall how difficult the simplest rebellions were. (I am struck now by the companionship of those who sit and ride for freedom; in my day, one who was disenchanted with segregation led a lonely, isolated life.) When I was a student at the University of Mis-sissippi and working part-time for a public opinion survey, I was sent on one occasion to interview the principal of a Negro school. I resolved to call him "Mister," an automatic courtesy had he been white, of course, but a title no white person ever used in addressing any Negro. The Southern code recognizes that a teacher should not be called "Boy" or "Uncle" or addressed by his first name, and so it prescribes the use of "Professor." This is a weasel word, which tells the Negro listener at once that the white Southerner knows the Negro man is educated and entitled to respect, but is nevertheless addressing him as an inferior who must keep his place. I was naïve enough then to think that if you only knew the right thing to do, you would do it easily and confidently. I was therefore surprised at my own fearfulness, for I firmly believed I was right. To myself I practiced over and over asking for "Mr. X." At the last moment, confronted by the strange dark faces of four or five men teachers in the school, I felt my courage desert me entirely and I asked for "Professor X." I am still haunted by the contempt that flooded the eyes of these strangers as I spoke. A dedicated segregationist would never have looked so directly in their eyes, of course, and so would have noticed only the familiar subservient politeness with which they gave me directions. I must have conducted the interview, but I remember nothing about it. I do recall that afterward I was so miserable and ashamed that I longed for someone with whom I could speak, but I could not admit to my tradition-minded friends that I had tried to call a Negro "Mister," or to my few friends among Northern liberals that I had failed. (At that time, I knew no Southern liberals, but I'm not sure I would have felt like talking to them about my failure either.) It was primarily fear that made this failure: the unreasoning terror that surrounds the breaking of any taboo, the fear of being ridiculous, perhaps fear of how the Negroes might respond to me if I stepped out of the familiar patterns, fear of what would happen if I openly declared my rejection of the South's way of life.

And here, I think, lies a partial reason why so many people conform outwardly to a system in which they inwardly disbelieve. Belief without action, belief that exists only in one's own mind, is too private to be quite real. Belief not uniformly and publicly expressed is not quite belief, for it has stood no test; a commitment that exists only in one's mind is not a commitment at all. Even the most public declarations may not always be supported by compatible actions, of course, but the purely private belief is vulnerable, can always be suspended or violated or postponed, just this one time, under these special circumstances.

When one's private belief is pushed toward public expression amid hostility, it may be modified or even annulled in ways one does not anticipate or even wholly understand or relish. (The "workshop" sessions that prepared for sit-ins and Freedom Rides probably served to minimize this diluting effect.) We are absolutely free to "believe" in private, but public avowal is another matter, not purely because of cowardice, but also because of self-deception. Confront some dedicated-to-silence moderates with a situation in which no one *forces* them to practice segregation, and they will discover, in pain and surprise, that they are more segregation-minded than they had ever realized. On the other hand, those who say they will never comply with integration may some day be dismayed to discover themselves quietly submitting to what they now consider impossible. They conform already to quite un-Southern rules of behavior if they go North, or into the Army, or abroad.

The pervasive influence of the "when-in-Rome" attitude in human affairs should not be underestimated, for this is the very stuff of which all kinds of social cohesion are largely constructed. The urge to conform, to meet the expectations of the others around us, runs deep in us all, and can be lightly denied by no one.

One of the difficulties between the traditional Southerner and the Northern liberal, however, is that neither side understands the other. Moreover, participants on both sides of the controversy persist in abandoning discussion of the only relevant issue (the civil right of Negroes) to dwell upon the oddities of those with whom they disagree. The average Northern liberal is quite unmoved by the South's defense of segregation as the morally correct way for the races to live. Unable to comprehend how this argument could be seriously believed, he simply blames it on undesirable character and ulterior motives. He has no grasp of the social functions of segregation or the enormity of the problems that will be created by its abolition. Thus the Northern liberal goes into argument with the Southerner in defense of the black man, but emerges with epithets for the white Southerner, whom he now calls stupid, lazy, apathetic, ignorant, ill-informed, hypocritical, arrogant, Negro-hating, provincial, sadistic, immoral.

The white Southerner, unmoved by the North's denunciation of segregation as immoral, observes correctly the Northerner's inconsistency, points out to him that he doesn't really mean what he says, and seldom grapples with any moral issue. This process is a highly effective distraction, and if we persist in it, the black man's rights can be forever lost in irrelevant acrimony between two kinds of white men.

The old-style picture of the Northern abolitionist at its kindest depicts him as boorish, meddling, ignorant, a fool, unrefined, misguided ("in the North too long" if a Southerner); or, less kindly, as hypocritical and maliciously hostile to the South. Increasingly, that last is the accepted portrait, with the added fillip that the integrationist must be either a dupe or a conscious agent of Communist powers, and that this whole thing is part of a Russian plot to overrun the United States.

Perhaps no charge made by the Southerner is less comprehensible to the Northern liberal mind. Is there any way we can understand how persons having sound minds and good intelligence can believe that the Northerner is an agent of the Reds? Let us try to leave the epithets and pseudo-psychology aside and take one another's arguments seriously enough at least to understand what we each know in advance we cannot accept.

The Northerner should understand this about the South: the impending loss of the color bar threatens to leave the South without any well-established, clearly understood basis for distinguishing the social positions of its members. No matter what forces eventually bring an end to segregation in the South, however, we need not expect that there will ever be indiscriminate mingling of middle, upper, and lower classes. (This mingling did not follow, on any great scale, even the social chaos of early Reconstruction days, though some lower class Negroes actually did hold political office for brief periods.) The Southerners fear that nothing less than the complete razing of the whole social structure is being demanded by barbaric outsiders; this fear is the emotional basis for the Southern charge of "Communism" that is so incomprehensible to the Northern ear.

For the South generally, the present caste system probably still makes fewer "mistakes" of classification than do social divisions based on wealth. This situation is rapidly changing, however. Many of the "fine old families," penniless for generations, are beginning to profit from the South's industrial expansion. Even in the deepest, most segregated South, it is for the first time in my recollection becoming a matter for embarrassment if one does not have money for the expected accouterments of his social position. But should we not do well to preserve the post-Civil War South's scorn of money and material possessions? There is something admirable in a spirit that values the soft voice and gentle manner of a lady but never notices the shabby dress she wears. Surely some of the traditions of family loyalty are worth saving too: the warmth of membership in an extended family group, the sisterliness of close cousins, the feelings of kinship and of belonging to a people and a region. The popularity of Southern novels indicates that not only the South, but the nation and the world, find pleasure and fascination in reading about these networks of personal relationship which are the heart of daily life in the deep South.

But when a lady cannot be acknowledged as one because her skin is dark, when the fact that one is the judge's first cousin is a more important piece of evidence than the testimony of eye witnesses, when the vicious killers of innocent persons must be protected by the Southern code—then some people in anger and outrage would dismiss the whole Southern system without another thought.

As for Southerners, many find it incomprehensible that the North has a legitimate interest in what they regard as purely a Southern matter. When one considers, however, the numbers of persons annually migrating from the South to other parts of the country, and the numbers of Northern businesses opening Southern branches, it is clear that the South's affairs have an impact upon the whole nation. The South, moreover, sends to every state of the nation an alarming number of minds so warped by prejudice as to be incapable of reflective or scientific thought: whites emotionally disfigured by arrogance and intemperance, Negroes scarred by their inner struggles with that ugly side of human nature which emerges in all peoples who are degraded and abased. The inability of the unreconstructed Southern mind to cope adequately with the simple demands of reality is perhaps nowhere better illustrated than in the frantic efforts of Southern legislators to turn time back upon itself and re-enter the last century.

There can be no doubt but that a majority of Americans, the country over, want to end both the worst aspects of segregation in the schools and the political disenfranchisement of the Southern Negro, however mixed may be their feelings about residential segregation and membership in private clubs. Despite this national majority, the South is attempting to ignore a decision that many had supposed passed into history with the end of the Civil War. The outcome of that war was essentially a decisive victory for the point of view that a nationwide majority takes precedence over the wishes of any state or region, regardless of the unanimity of opinion within that state or region.

Southern whites will probably very soon be forced to stop using public facilities, paid for with tax money, as if they were their own private property. Therefore, every new public construction in the South should be undertaken in the realization that within a few years it will be used by whites and Negroes together. Most facilities will need more staff when they receive more use; perhaps there is a need for the expansion of public parks, libraries, hospitals, and the like, even greater than the need for new schools.

In the next few years, also, Southern whites must no doubt face some unsettling facts. For example, whites living in the few counties of Mississippi that are 90 per cent Negro and 10 per cent white will some time have to admit that Negroes are entitled to about 90 per cent of the public offices there. The greater the harshness of the whites in defending their usurped powers in these last days of struggle, the greater the chance that when the Negroes eventually do get the political power to which they are entitled, they may be as harsh as the whites.

One immediate advantage to the white South in early integration lies in the fact that the Negro community is still marked by rifts and division. Should Negroes receive the vote now, Negro bloc voting would probably be rare. But if integration in the South comes late and largely as a consequence of such demonstrations as Freedom Rides and sit-ins, the Negro group will have consolidated, sealed over its divisions, and become a unified force, a racially defined, cohesive group tightly organized for political action, likely to vote as a bloc in all elections. If, in order to obtain basic human rights, the Negroes have to develop this much solidarity as a specifically Negro group, the stage will be set for continuing generations of white vs. black struggle, and it will be difficult for psychological integration ever to occur. Many thoughtful minds, among both white and black, are weary of race, and would like to be simply human, free to devote their energies to matters of more enduring significance.

The South's only real choice now is whether to plan and act while it is still relatively early in the game, or whether to keep struggling, resisting, refusing to plan, until too late—until all power of choice is taken away. The waiting, struggling South will see that power vanish. It will be taken away by the Federal Government, by the Negroes, by overidealistic liberals who imagine the cotton fields peopled exclusively with oppressed Ralph Bunches and Leontyne Prices, and who do not realize the frightening extent to which the white South has succeeded in creating, if not always the Frankenstein-like monster of "black savagery" it gibbers about, at least a wary group of ill-educated, emotionally impoverished people who have to learn the responsibilities and privileges of first-class citizenship.

If the South forces a second Reconstruction upon itself, it will not end as before with a quiet restitution of white privilege: it will be a permanent and total loss not only of white supremacy, but of many worthy and valuable attributes of the Southern heritage. The white South can be absolutely certain of bringing about the complete destruction of its present social life if it persists in massive resistance.

At this stage, one can only guess what a "new South" will be. Laws will be taken more seriously, for they will be an increasingly important part of the community's safeguards. (It is a long step forward in civilization when Mississippi arrests the Freedom Riders instead of assaulting them.) Friendship or kinship will no longer be decisive in legal contest, for there will be a growing replacement of the rule of privilege with the rule of law. All men, white and dark, will show an increased self-esteem, as they increasingly take pride in their skills, abilities, and knowledge, and decreasingly consider color as a measure of a man's worth. And I hope that the new South will have found some way to preserve its traditional view that what lies in a man's heart is more significant than what lies in his pocket.

A DECADE OF DECISION

Thomas D. Clark . . .

Professor of American History and chairman of the Department of History at the University of Kentucky; has served as visiting professor at Harvard University, the University of Chicago, and the University of Wisconsin; former president of the Southern Historical Association and of the Mississippi Valley Historical Association; former editor of the *Journal of Southern History;* author of *The Kentucky River, Frontier America,* and *The Emerging South.*

A subject of foremost consideration in the Southern Governors' Conference in 1961 was the economic and social status of the South as reflected in the current census report. Before the facts revealed in this report were known, regional economists were warning that the South had not made as much actual progress in industrialization as appeared to be the case in a surface view. The fact was that many industrial plants that had moved South had employed only the most acceptable Southern laborers and had left the less desirable ones to shift for themselves as best they could in a highly competitive search for jobs. A closer look further revealed that the region had not made as much industrial progress as Southerners believed it had.

Cast against the background of southern economic history since 1920, the South has undergone a tremendously fundamental revolution, but cast against the background of change in the nation it was doubtful that the region was doing more than holding its own. If it is to make the necessary gains that are to place it in a competitive position between now and the end of the century, it will have to make tremendous strides in this decade.

In the spring and summer of 1961 two southern states received widespread and damaging publicity because of the violence caused by the Freedom Riders. This new effort to destroy the barrier of racial discrimination in travel facilities caught Alabama and Mississippi by surprise. In these states attention had been focused on the more pressing issues of desegregation of public schools and the granting of Negroes free access to the polls. These were issues that offered the most serious threat to what some Southerners have called "the Southern way of life." These were also the issues that were emphasized in the first voluminous report of the Civil Rights Commission.

The Interstate Commerce Commission had ruled a decade earlier that discriminatory barriers should be removed in interstate travel. But some states chose to thwart the ruling either by ignoring it or by permitting its violation, and it had been considered largely in its application to railways, not buses. Desegregation of airline facilities occurred early, and Negroes rode interstate trains across the South. They slept in pullman cars, ate in diners, and had full access to other passenger accommodations. On the airlines Negroes traveled without difficulty. The Atlanta airport, for instance, was long ago desegregated without incident. True, relatively small numbers of

Negroes traveled by air, but those who did had no racial difficulty.

When the Freedom Riders set out, they went almost unnoticed in their journey through at least four of the other Southern states. Only when they reached Alabama and Mississippi did they face trouble. Two facts are important. The Freedom Riders who went by bus to Alabama were attacking discrimination in the facilities where the great majority of Negroes traveled, and where they come in the most direct association with white people of a lower economic and social scale. Second, they came South on the avowed mission of actively challenging the practice of racial discrimination in interstate travel. Subsequently the fight was transferred to Mississippi, but not before state officials had an opportunity to prevent the violent mob action that had shocked Alabama and the nation. In Mississippi the first twenty-seven Freedom Riders, and those who followed them, accepted jail sentences rather than abandon their crusade. They were arrested on charges of breach of the peace for disobeying an officer. In the following September the Interstate Commerce Commission reasserted and broadened its original ruling ordering desegregation of interstate travel. This time the Attorney General of the United States took an active hand in pressing for such action.

No one but the most uninformed extremist believed Alabama and Mississippi would be allowed to continue discrimination in interstate travel. All the world learned about the shocking mob action in Alabama especially and the failure of that state's governor to take a positive hand in suppressing it. The Mississippi officials prevented mob action, but they permitted one wave after another of Freedom Riders to arrive in Jackson and be arrested on breach of the peace charges, and then be carted off to the state penitentiary at Parchman because the jails in Jackson were overcrowded.

These overt racial acts, plus the highly unfavorable publicity, caused thoughtful Southerners to take a closer look at the plight of the South. The president of the Alabama Chamber of Commerce thought his state had received a black eye that it would be a long time forgetting. Business leaders throughout the South quickly realized that though the great portion of the region enjoyed racial peace, and was actually making limited progress in racial adjustments, the area as a whole suffered. Alabama and Mississippi were labeled the "South," and many outsiders were unable to make intelligent distinction between the two states and the region as a whole.

Earlier, Clinton, Tennessee, Little Rock, and New Orleans had experienced damaging upheavals over token school desegregation. Mob outbursts in these places were stimulated and led largely by persons who were either incapable of taking or unwilling to take a long-range look at the South at this moment in the twentieth century. Perhaps a more fundamental reaction to token integration was the closing of public schools in Prince Edward County, Virginia. Here people took a step to hamper educational effort at a time when the American people were being urged to make greater educational effort to preserve civilization itself. In areas torn by strife both the people and their political leaders had focused on the single narrow purpose of keeping all Negroes out of Southern white public schools. The Citizens' Councils and other extremist organizations had preached the doctrine that token admissions of Negroes to the white schools would destroy all social and economic barriers.

Not one of the howling mobs in Clinton, Little Rock, New Orleans, or Montgomery saw that a violent outbreak would have such deep economic meaning for the very people who were fomenting violence. A major purpose of the great effort to bring about large-scale economic conversion in the South was that of absorbing the energy of the accumulated pool of labor. William P. Engel, president of an important Alabama real estate firm, said, "Unfortunately, it's just those people for whom we're spending time and money to bring in industry to provide work who are causing all the trouble."

Quickly the effects of the unfortunate incident of Little Rock reflected its disastrous meaning in the failure of Arkansas to attract desperately needed new industries to the state. Voicing the hopes of their state, two Alabama businessmen said they thought that the violent outbreak over the Freedom Riders in May, 1961, would not disrupt industrial expansion. The *Wall Street Journal* replied:

> If the experience of Little Rock and the rest of the state of Arkansas is any indication, however, the optimism of these two Alabamians is not likely to be borne out. In Little Rock, industrial development skidded to a halt after the flare-up over school integration in 1957. The Arkansas capital city had attracted an average of five new plants a year ranging in value from $100,000 to $3,000,000 between 1950-1957. In the early months of 1957, before the outbreak of violence, eight new plants were opened. But according to Everett Tucker, director of Little Rock's industrial development commission, in the nearly four years since the start of the school troubles, there has not been "a single major industrial expansion."

Industrial expansion in Arkansas fell from $131,000,000 in 1956 to $25,250,000 in 1958.

In times of dramatic violence the Ku Klux Klan has shown its ugly head. Its members appeared in the upheaval at Anniston and Montgomery over the Freedom Riders. Some held a rally in Atlanta protesting the desegregation of schools in September, 1961, and others met in Dallas, Texas, at the same time. Occasionally Klansmen flog people, they burn crosses, and otherwise foment trouble. United States District Judge Frank M. Johnson, Jr., charged three Alabama Klan organizations with causing the commotions in the Alabama bus stations. In twentieth-century America the appearance of the Ku Klux Klan is a fundamental contradiction of the nation's democratic commitments. Its membership is cowardly, and no doubt ignorant. Its leaders are self-seeking and indifferent to the general welfare of the country, but it is doubtful that this cancerous organization now exerts any significant political influence anywhere in the South. A positive leadership in the executive offices in states where it flourishes would no doubt destroy it.

Of far more importance in the South is the attitude of Southern political, educational, civic, and business leaders. While extremists after 1954 were shouting "never," the moderate-minded leaders in the South believed that a change was inevitable in the Southern way of life. While most of them might have chosen another course, they intended to respect the laws of the nation. Basically this element of Southern leadership is both conservative and slow to act. Although it waited too long to exert its influence, it has acted. This fact is reflected in the peaceful school openings in the fall of 1961. Atlanta, Dallas, Memphis, New Orleans, and Nashville opened schools with some desegregated classes and without dramatic incident. In every case there had been careful planning, and the decision was made to enforce the law with local policemen. Southerners in these cities were determined there would be no more Little Rock and New Orleans blunders to besmirch their good reputations.

It is true, of course, that only limited numbers of Negro children were admitted into the newly desegregated schools, and these were chosen after a most rigorous screening. It is also true that there are areas in the South where no steps have been taken, nor are any planned, to conform with the Supreme Court's ruling. But these areas notwithstanding, there is too much intent to obey the law in most of the South to permit new trouble spots from causing more than local difficulty. There is no longer any indication that the South as a region can be unified to resist a rule of the central government. Governors Ross Barnett and John Patterson seemed to have discovered this fact in their efforts to formulate a "unity" program on questions of states' rights, sovereignty, and economies. Their fellow governors showed no intent of co-operating in such a move when they met in Nashville.

In some areas parents can boycott schools, or close the schools altogether, as they have done in Prince Edward County, Virginia. They can even open private schools. But the history of education in the South is such that one could hardly predict a brilliant future for classless private schools. A good example is the difficulties that promoters of the private school movement in New Orleans are having in obtaining sufficient funds to finance their project. The educational challenge in the South is so great at this point that any interference in or disruption of the public schools would be disastrous. Fortunately there are enough people with foresight and common sense to understand that this is so. On April 14, 1961, the Georgia Parents-Teachers Association met in Albany, Georgia. Mrs. B. A. Watensky of the small town of Fernbank introduced three resolutions, which were passed without heat or debate. These asked that (1) there be a firm enforcement of local laws, (2) that communities under court order be prepared for desegregation by discussion and planning, and (3) that civic, youth, and church organizations prepare communities for peaceful desegregation. The three federal judges ruling in *Hall et al. v. St.* on August 30, 1961, stated more succinctly than anyone else the South's educational situation. "This," they said, "is not the moment in history for a state to experiment with ignorance. When it does, it must expect close scrutiny of the experiment."

Education is one of the present South's most urgent needs. Compared with its past record, education in the region has made phenomenal advance since 1945. Compared with educational advance in the nation, however, the South is perhaps failing to hold its own with even some of its past achievements. The North Carolina Advisory Committee on Civil Rights in its report in 1960 on "Equal Protection of the Law in Education in North Carolina" reached the conclusion that "the Southeast is the most uneducated part of the United States." Their report left little doubt in the minds of North Carolinians as to the status of their educational effort.

While North Carolinians were licking their wounds over this report, complacent Kentuckians were being jarred by two searching reports on their schools. Not only did these reports reflect an unsatisfactory level of educational achievement in far too many of the state's schools. They reflected also the insidiousness of partisan political practices in the state's educational system. A similar report for other Southern states might reveal a comparable condition. The sternness of such reports is reflected in the fact that the South no longer battles basic illiteracy, but functional illiteracy as well. Although Southern congressmen and senators have consistently joined forces with opponents of federal aid to education, they are not oblivious to the fact that such aid is all but mandatory if the South is to make the educational progress necessary if it is to become competitive with the rest of the nation.

In higher education, the South has made phenomenal progress in the past two decades. Here again, however, the region has failed to keep pace with the advances made in the nation. In an era when graduate study and research are being emphasized, Southern universities and colleges are finding it difficult to raise their standards, hire capable staff members, construct expensive buildings, and maintain research facilities. Yet the new way of life in the South demands that institutions of higher learning supply a major portion of the personnel employed by industries operating in the region. Historically Southerners have looked upon the sciences as purely academic branches of learning. Today specialized training in the sciences is mandatory if the South is to improve itself economically.

Any state that allows its program of higher education to be disrupted for any reason is pursuing a foolhardy and disastrous course. The people of Georgia and their public officials indicated they believed this to be true in their complete reversal of stand in regard to the desegregation of the University of Georgia and the Georgia Institute of Technology. To have allowed an emotional upheaval over desegregation to halt work in these institutions would have resulted in irreparable harm for all the foreseeable future.

Graduate education of high quality is a major issue before the present South. Not a single university in the region is in a competitive position with the top dozen or so institutions in the country. To achieve this position, a Southern school will have to add material strength in mature faculty, laboratory facilities, and library holdings. This is not to say, however, that graduate education is neglected in the region. There are good libraries, good laboratories, and good faculties, but they are too limited to reach the goals that the South must achieve if it is to prosper. Statistical studies from several Southern states have been made to prove that they "are improving the handling of education," but Dean W. Gordon Whaley of the University of Texas Graduate School says, "I have read much of the material and I still must take the position that so far as we are concerned with the real core proposition, the superior development of the mind, the South ranks in second-, third-, and fourth-rate categories."

There are many resources in abundance in the South. Some of them are poorly exploited; some have been wastefully handled; others need careful management to be profitable. There is no resource, however, which does not demand the most intelligent and skillful use. This requires superior technical training of exploiters and consumers. In no field have parts of the South reversed traditional practices more than in the management and production of forest resources. Since 1930, when pulpwood was scarcely listed in regional statistics, the South has become a major pulp paper producing area of the country. In 1960 it supplied almost 60 per cent of the pulp paper produced in the United States. Each year this industrial potential grows. Hundreds of thousands of acres of exhausted and eroded lands are being planted to trees, and the profession of forester has become a major calling.

Just as old fields have been snatched from briars, persimmon bushes, sage grass, and gullies and made productive of timber, Southerners have come to look upon water as a key resource. Phenomenal progress has been made in water conservation, progress that ranges all the way from the construction of small head stream ponds to the vast reservoirs of the Tennessee Valley Authority. Early in the 1920's water was associated with the generation of electric power. Now it is also widely associated with transportation, irrigation, recreation, and flood controls. No longer is the Tennessee Valley the scene of devastating floods, and farmlands in this valley have increased their productivity phenomenally. The increase of corn production is more than 100 per cent, and other grains make much greater yields.

Not all the improvement of soils management in the South is to be attributed to flood and water control. The South's manufacture and application of adequate amounts of commercial fertilizers have revolutionized crop production. In the last thirty years Southerners generally have become aware of the importance of soil analyses and are following scientific advice in bringing their lands into full production. Again, the region is developing its livestock industry. Diseases have been brought under control, old cotton lands have been planted to grass, and local markets have been established for the sale of livestock.

The exploitation of land resource by modern mechanical methods has resulted in a fairly significant increase in the size of farms. For the first time the Southern farmer must be as aware of cost of production and margin of profit as a manufacturer or a banker. Before he can farm efficiently he has to have access to enough land to justify a sizable outlay for machines. Nevertheless, the mechanization of the Southern farm has resulted in large-scale social displacement. Though tenant farming has not been abandoned, the nature of this type of farming has changed, and the number of tenants reduced to only a fraction of the total in 1930. When a Southern farmer buys a new medium-sized tractor with the necessary equipment for modern farming, he displaces at least two families who would have been employed under the old system. Even after the great migration away from Southern farms, some economists say, still larger numbers of people could move away and actually improve conditions.

Southerners possess not only water, land, timber, and grass; they also have a vast fuel resource in coal, natural gas, and oil. If predictions of future fuel shortages have any validity, the coal-bearing regions, especially in the Appalachian South, hold a future promise for the industrial nation. In fact it is not necessary to wait for the future; a major portion of both electric and atomic energy are produced by the heavy use of coal. The Tennessee Valley Authority steam plants alone are top consumers of Southern coal. Coal mining, like farming, however, has become a highly mechanized industry and the tragedy of social displacement is a stark one. The old hand-miner no longer finds employment for his trade, and unhappily he is unfitted for any other; thus he has become socially dependent upon public support, and he has turned much of the Appalachian South into an area of crisis.

As the South has undergone changes in agriculture, and in the overwhelmingly rural pattern of its mode of life, it has become more a region of suburban and urban communities. Southern cities have grown rapidly since 1930, creating the metropolitan centers such as those about Atlanta, Dallas, Louisville, Birmingham, Miami, Richmond, and Petersburg. More industrial centers are arising about what were once sleepy cotton or staple towns such as Charleston, Natchez, Decatur in Alabama, Paducah, and Lake Charles in Louisiana. As these metropolitan and urban centers expand, the base of Southern social relationships is changed radically. In social organization, community services, law enforcement, race relations, and politics, suburban Southerners have been quick to depart from Southern traditions of demagoguery and red-necked political exploitation.

The urban Southerner will probably make his greatest threat upon traditional political organization. The time is at hand for a widespread revolt by urban-dwelling Southerners against the discriminatory country legislators and governors in the state houses. Already citizens of Nashville, Tennessee, have taken their revolt against the rural legislator and his flagrant gerrymanderings to the United States Supreme Court, and it is significant that these rebellious Southerners have been joined by urban dwellers elsewhere in the nation. A historian can be a prophet long enough to say that the favorable court decision in this issue, rendered early in 1962, will no doubt bring a reversal of political procedures in the state houses, and the old-style politician will join the hand cotton picker and crosstie wagon in the junk yard of the past.

Southern politicians of the traditional stripe face other assaults. Surely none but the blindest white supremacist can fail to see that the time is at hand when the Negro will be a free participant in Southern political affairs. The findings of the Civil Rights Commission are indicative enough that barriers that kept Negroes from the polls will be removed either by stronger civil rights legislation or by court action. In no area of its traditional social relationships does the South face greater pressure of unfavorable national public opinion than in its outdated attempts to keep the Negro from voting. Conversely, the Negro can make no more significant immediate gains than by obtaining free access to the vote. Currently Southern Negroes are being worked up to the pitch of camp-meeting fervor to register and vote. Once this is done, Southern political leadership will be far less inflammatory or irresponsible in its public utterances and actions, and there will be a marked reduction in the unfortunate incidents that occurred because governors and law enforcement officials failed to meet their responsibilities.

One must not conclude that because of extremist actions in

Alabama, Georgia, Mississippi, and Louisiana, the Negro is without the vote in other states. In all the furore over flagrant discrimination in those four states, one is apt to forget that Negroes are free to register and vote in South Carolina, even if there are still islands of intimidation, and they are free to vote in most of the other Southern states.

Politically, parts of the South toss about in troubled beds. There is at present a wave of conservatism. A Republican was elected to the United States Senate from Texas, a Republican state representative was sent to the South Carolina Legislature from Richland County, and a Republican was elected mayor of Mobile. It may be that the new industry in the South has brought a rising Republican support to the region, but it is far more likely that the majorities cast for Republican candidates were protest votes: votes that reflected a general unrest and dissatisfaction with many things. There is, however, no indication that the South is going Republican at any time in the immediate future; rather it will try desperately to remain conservative and conform with its political traditions.

In a comprehensive view of the South in the past decade these considerations seem to be indicative of the way the region is changing: First, it is clearly evident that much more rapid industrialization will have to occur before it can compete with the rest of the country. Second, although the Negro has left the South in large numbers, he has now pretty well stabilized his number in the South, and his number is still a significant part of the Southern population. Some responsible social and economic leadership has come to accept the fact that to leave this part of the region's population productively inferior and in a state of ignorance is to imprison the South permanently at the bottom in national statistical tables, and further to sink the region in social and economic difficulty. Third, the Southern agricultural economy has experienced a revolution that has left little of either old Southern attitudes or methods in existence. And, fourth, Southerners have come to think of themselves less as people of an isolated region, and now view their problems more in the matrix of national and international relationships.

The South is still a long way from removing its traditional racial barriers. There are still rough hurdles ahead, but even so some main ones have been negotiated. The Border States have made genuine progress in desegregating all sorts of public facilities. Schools have been desegregated, and in some cities such as Louisville and Washington, Negro teachers have been employed. Both the University of Georgia and Georgia Institute of Technology have admitted Negro students; Duke University has made a timid beginning in this direction; its neighbor, the University of North Carolina, opened its doors to Negroes earlier. The borderland universities of Kentucky, Missouri, Maryland, and Oklahoma have had no unpleasant incidents with their Negro students. There are no indications that any former all-white public school in the South will ever be overrun by Negroes, or that such associations will result in the social calamities predicted in extremist literature.

Again, the Southern Governors' Conference in Nashville, Tennessee, in the fall of 1961, reflected clearly that its members mean to pursue a course of moderation. For a third time this body passed over Governor Orval Faubus of Arkansas as Chairman, even though he was its senior member. Even the "unity" move advocated by three governors was ignored. Responsible Southerners are in no mood to argue academic questions in the face of the economic and social realities revealed in the new census report. Most of the governors knew that a growing body of their constituents were determined to make major improvements in the Southern educational effort, not disrupt it, and that there was a rapidly developing core of economic realists who were equally as determined to be done with mobs and violent outbreaks and to get on with exploiting regional resources as intelligently as possible. South-erners may not like some of the changes that have occurred. A majority of them would like to cling to many of their old sentiments and attitudes, but they have become realists in the past decades. There is no old South to return to, and the future South struggles against mighty odds to transform itself in its twentieth-century revolution.

If the South is to move forward during the rest of the twentieth century it will do so in education, conservation, management of resources, banking, industry, politics, and mechanized agriculture. Its first concern will be with ac-complishing the fullest possible utilization of all its human energies. Political progress will have to be made positively. The region cannot possibly hope to achieve social and eco-nomic progress if its state and congressional leadership persists in following a negative course on issues that affect vitally some of the educational, social, and industrial fields. Finally, it is somewhat irrelevant to talk so loudly about sovereignty and state's rights for public consumption when Southern leadership knows that until the South can produce and control a greater portion of the necessary capital to finance changes, there will always be a dependence on outside public and private re-sources.

THE GREAT OPPORTUNITY

Lenoir Chambers . . .

Native of Charlotte, N.C.; graduate, University of North Carolina, and student, Columbia University School of Journalism; infantry lieutenant, France and Germany, 1917-19; News Bureau Director, University of North Carolina; staff, Greensboro, N.C., *Daily News*, 1921-29; associate editor, Norfolk *Virginian-Pilot*, 1929-44; editor, Norfolk *Ledger-Dispatch*, 1944-50; editor, *The Virginian Pilot*, now retired; member of the American Society of Newspaper Editors, National Conference of Editorial Writers; winner of the Pulitzer Prize for editorial writing in 1960, for editorials on school closings in Virginia and other segregation problems in Virginia and the South; author of *Stonewall Jackson* (two volumes), 1959.

The decisive fact confronting the Southern States in May of 1954 and again in May of 1955 was that the Supreme Court, in effect, had convicted them of unconstitutional discrimination in the operation of their public school systems. It had directed them to change these racial practices.

This is an awkward position for States to be caught in. Although the turbulence of the succeeding years has made many men forget it, the Supreme Court was aware of the probelms and difficulties in changes of great social depth—even if it did not possess the genius to foresee all of them—that compliance with its decisions would entail. In its hearings of the cases embodied in *Brown v. Board of Education*, the court invited the participation of the attorney general of the United States and the attorneys general of other States besides those involved directly in the litigation. It posed questions which it said it would like to have answered for its guidance. It separated the decision in principle (1954) and the decision as to compliance (1955) by a full year in order that the nature of the changes might sink in and that all people—perhaps starting with the court itself—might have time to think about what should come next.

Before arriving at the decision as to compliance, the court again invited answers to questions about specific lines of action on which it desired advice. After arriving at the decision as to compliance, the Supreme Court directed the district courts to make arrangements in accordance with conditions that varied from State to State. (There are many Souths.) It is a rare issue that discloses the Supreme Court showing so much concern about how to give reality to what it had concluded the Constitution required.

This judicial concern could not lessen materially the formidable extent of the Southern embarrassment. Everyone knew that deep changes were in progress in Southern life. But the public assumptions and the political commitments still prevailing in many parts of the South had not advanced far beyond Ulrich Bonnell Phillips' definition of the unifying principle and central theme of Southern history: that the South "shall be and remain a white man's country."

Yet here was the Supreme Court saying in its 1954 decision that "in the field of public education the doctrine of 'separate but equal' has no place" because "separate educational facilities are inherently unequal." And here was the court saying in its

1955 decision that "the [Federal] courts will require that the defendants make a prompt and reasonable start toward full compliance" with the 1954 ruling.

The Supreme Court had arrived at these conclusions by unanimous votes. Justice Harlan succeeded Justice Jackson between the 1954 and 1955 decisions, and the total for the two decisions is ten justices. Three other justices who have taken their seats on the court since May, 1955, have participated in subsequent decisions growing out of the two basic decisions, with no indication of unhappiness over the court's record. In all, then, thirteen Supreme Court justices made the original decisions, or accepted them, or amplified them in detail. None has ever dissented.

It is still the fashion in some quarters to attribute these decisions and this unanimity to the influence of Chief Justice Warren. Those who say "the Warren court" rarely smile when they say it. But this is plainly a political interpretation, not based in its derogatory intent on fact or reasoning.

Chief Justice Warren took his seat on the court on October 3, 1953. When he read the decision in *Brown v. Board of Education* on May 17, 1954, he had been a member of the court for seven and a half months. Earlier he had been a State attorney general, a governor, and a candidate for vice president. He was not without public influence. But the Supreme Court had been considering these cases since 1952. It had made decisions in higher education cases that pointed in the same direction. Its justices are perennially characterized by independence, individualism, depth of conviction, pride of opinion, and even touches of prima donna-ism. Over the decades the court may tend to follow the election returns, as the Dooley dictum postulated, but any supposition that it scrambles into line behind the chief justice—*any* chief justice —has no evidence to support it.

More specifically, you engage in pure fantasy if you suppose that Earl Warren could pull around by the nose Hugo Black, Stanley F. Reed, Felix Frankfurter, William O. Douglas, Robert H. Jackson, Harold H. Burton, Tom C. Clark, Sherman Minton, and John Marshall Harlan, and in later years William J. Brennan, Jr., Charles E. Whittaker, and Potter Stewart. If there was a case against the decisions, it would have to rest on something more substantial than tall talk about the chief justice's machinations or his personal or official dominance over the brains and backbones of his associates.

Was there anything more substantial in the objections to the ruling? The list of allegations is long: The Supreme Court had no jurisdiction in educational matters. The court had already settled the segregation issue in *Plessy v. Ferguson* (1896), the "separate but equal" doctrine of which later was extended to school situations. The court had no "right" to reverse this decision fifty-eight years later. When the court rested its decision on the Fourteenth Amendment it relied on an amendment that had not been ratified constitutionally and ought now to be wrenched out of the Constitution. The court had produced no constitutional basis or reasoning for a judgment that "separate educational facilities are inherently unequal." The court had proclaimed its lack of legal justification when it cited social philosophers in a footnote, especially Gunnar Myrdal, who had written some uncomplimentary judgments about Southern institutions and about the Constitution itself. And so on.

Most of these attacks plainly lack the force of fact or logic. If the Constitution does not speak specifically of education, it declares specifically that "no state shall make or enforce *any law* which shall abridge the privileges or immunities of citizens of the United States . . . *nor deny to any person* within its jurisdiction the equal protection of the laws." (The italics are supplied.) That broad limitation on the States has often been held to be of sufficient authority for the courts to prohibit State action of many kinds. Clearly the States cannot step over such limits without inviting judicial rebuke.

Nor can protesters grant jurisdiction to the Supreme Court in *Plessy v. Ferguson,* thereby accepting the court's authority to lay down the "separate but equal" doctrine, without granting to the court jurisdiction in a case brought to overturn the doctrine of "separate but equal." If the court could consider the one, it could consider the other.

Nor is it possible to ignore the fact that the Supreme Court has been reversing itself cheerfully from far back in its history, often with the approval of revered exemplars of judicial wisdom among its members. In two cases, one in 1932 and the other in 1944, the court itself counted forty overrulings that it had made of earlier decisions.

An academic argument might be made about the manner in which the Fourteenth Amendment was ratified. But that amendment had stood up for eighty-six years (ninety-four years now), and the 1960's are a little late for overturning the American Civil War of the 1860's. People who argue Calhoun in the age of Kennedy do so, necessarily, in the spirit of those who debate what would have happened at Gettysburg if Stonewall Jackson had been there. The issue has its points as a conversation piece, but it does not have much reality.

The substance of the constitutional argument in the 1954 decision, the heart of the question of whether separate educational facilities in the public schools create unconstitutional discrimination, can be argued a long time and no doubt will be. But it will be argued, I think, with less and less conviction as more and more of the old lines of segregation in Southern life are worn thin from much crossing over and prove difficult to trace, and eventually are obliterated altogether.

Gunnar Myrdal is a welcome whipping horse, but not much more, for those who forget that a Supreme Court justice has cited Herbert Spencer's *Social Statics* without being found in contempt of judicial propriety.

The decision is the thing: (1) the practical fact that the Supreme Court did so rule and, for a persuasive note, that it ruled unanimously and thus far with thirteen justices agreeing; (2) the constitutional fact that a Supreme Court decision has weight and cannot be tossed aside at will: that, in the words of the court itself, "the vitality of these constitutional principles cannot be allowed to yield simply because of disagreement with them"; and (3) the legal fact that the decision is the law. It is a serious matter under the American system to violate, systematically derogate, continually belittle, publicly defy, and thereby encourage wholesale disobedience of clearly established judicial rulings.

To these must be added the political fact that the decision accords in principle with what most Americans regard as a foundation of their treasured constitutionalism: the guarantee of equal protection for all Americans. A large majority of the American people unmistakably approve the decision as reasonable and desirable, as well as a constitutionally sound advance, in the strengthening of the American nation. If that were not so, the desperate search by Southern resisters for some clear-cut way to obviate the effects of the decision would have led to genuine attempts by constitutional means, legislative, amendatory, or elective, to alter one or more of the premises

upon which the decision rests. Many proposals for such purposes have been studied. All have been discarded. Nothing has
come of the efforts because all such steps would require
approval by a majority opinion that does not exist in American
life and shows no signs of coming into existence. It is not only
the courts, it is the votes, that are against the troubled South.

Votes, to be sure, have often been characterized in these
contentions as evidence of the political strength of Negro
residents of politically doubtful States in the North. In this
imperfect world the weight of bloc pressures of this kind may
have exerted influence. But that this is the controlling explanation for the American verdict is altogether improbable. Nor is
it reasonable to lay this charge against politicians in the North
who seek to change the *status quo* in the South and at the
same time to pass over those political actions in the South
which reflect a desire to maintain the *status quo*. The coin has
two sides.

No, the decision is in being, it has roots, it is here to stay,
and its application is spreading—not at a wild-fire pace certainly, and not at the same rate in all areas (for there are many
Souths), and as yet not at all, or scarcely at all, in some areas.
If the justices of the Supreme Court are moved to look across
the map of these changes, and of others clearly on the way,
they may look hard at what has not been done. But there may
be satisfactions too. The justices are entitled at least to the
recognition that, on the bare record of the manner in which
they approached their decision and arranged for its enforcement, they knew something of the minds and emotions that
they were upsetting in a region where many people—not all
of the stripe of the bully boys and the exploiting politicians
either—thought it wiser to maintain the historical traditions
and the older way of life.

The enforcement of the 1954 and 1955 decisions was certainly not going to be automatic. The resistance instinct saw to that: the instinct that was born of 246 years of slavery in America, the instinct that had been nurtured by the struggle to justify "the peculiar institution" and to find "positive good" in it, by the debate in logic and emotion with the abolitionists, by the concentration on the politics of Southern defense, by the American Civil War, by defeat, occupation, and political and economic inferiority—by all the forces that drove Southern life back upon itself and removed it from the main channels of American life and separated it in thought and feeling. It is impossible to understand the racial struggles of the 1950's without understanding the sectional struggles of the nineteenth century. The tremendous weight of heritage that the past has left piled upon the Southern back, bending it beyond any capacity of the South to keep pace with the nation and the world of which it is, nevertheless, inescapably a part—this is a burden of primary importance, as the Supreme Court recognized.

What much of the South had more difficulty in understanding was—and unfortunately in important degree still is—that this was a condition that was unsatisfactory in the modern world and could not and would not be tolerated forever. Specifically, it would not be tolerated by the world of today.

This is the fact that gives life and meaning and a future of promise to the Supreme Court's decisions. For the constitutionalism of the decisions, essential though it is for the legal foundations and for the guidance of the changes under respectable auspices, is by no means the limit of what the Supreme Court has established. The decisions have the additional effect, and in practicality the larger influence, of encouraging and opening the way for the operation of other forces that were already exerting their influence on life in the South and were certain to exercise more.

These are the forces that grow out of the spirit of the Twentieth Century at mid-point. They are life itself as we know it today. In substance they are nothing less than the United States of America, of which the South is a part. They are the world itself, of which the United States is a part. In the long run the South could never escape the impact of such forces. Now it has the opportunity to face them frankly and deal with them honestly, and thereby make the most of its own unrealized possibilities.

The old condition of discriminatory restrictions that could not and would not be tolerated by the modern world was unsatisfactory to American constitutionalism, as we have seen; and once the issue came up for fresh examination in the light of the Constitution in today's world, there could be no doubt of the decision. But it was unsatisfactory also to the American role in the world, from which the United States cannot escape and in which it must exert its influence, and must have an influence worthy of being exerted. It was unsatisfactory to the concept of unity in the development of American life—not the kind of unity that would smother regional individuality and lead to the death of the historical and traditional color and quality and attributes in the sections, but emphatically the kind of unity that would never sanction a retreat into isolationism within the nation. The development of American life could never rise to its potential heights if a great section of the nation lacked the capacity or the will to contribute its fair share. The South had contributed gloriously in the organization and early growth of the United States. For its own sake, and for the nation's, it would have to do so again.

If these goals seem a little removed—though they are not—

from the personal life of the South as it is lived in all the communities and homes where human beings work and laugh and weep, then let the issues be considered solely in terms of the regional life of the Negroes and the white people of the South. They are the ones who live side by side. They are affected first and deepest.

The moment the people of the South do this, they must face the truth that nothing—in the most literal sense, *not any thing* —can maintain the old conditions of life in the Southern States. The South stands in an era of historic transition that began long before the Supreme Court decisions of 1954 and 1955. It is the era of the coming of age of the American Negro citizenship, politically and economically; and it is proclaiming itself in all aspects of life in the South. There is no possible way of averting this transition. If no other influences assure its continuation, education would. The Southern States cannot send hundreds of thousands of Negro boys and girls to public schools every year, and tens of thousands of Negro young people to colleges and universities, without expecting, when university, college, or even high school courses are completed, that an increasing number of them will rise up and look around and ask, "Where do we stand in the scheme of things?"

Education alone would do it, but other influences pressing to the same end are numerous and powerful. They include all the means of communication, old and new; the national business and commercial operations that have no regard for sections, regions, or State borders, or for race, color, or creed; the lessons of war and the desegregation of the armed forces; the requirements of international leadership; the shifting tides of population; the achievements of Negroes in the arts and in sports; the objectivity of modern historians and the minds of modern writers.

Even influences that flow out of the life of America are not all. For the coming of age of the Negro citizenship of the United States coincides with the coming of independence and the rise of many new peoples around the globe. Their color, often dark, and their background as they have surged upward to seek national dignity, have had their influence on the thinking of American Negroes. The differences are deep and numerous, but the world movement and the movement within the United States (which has relied on American constitutional methods only) have not only come in the same era: they have reflected a spirit that is alive and vibrant in the world today. It would be remarkable if the one did not affect the other.

All such influences of modern life are operating to free Negro citizenship from the old restrictions of Southern inheritance—and often, it should be added, of Northern practice. To pretend that the rise of these citizens to their rightful place in American life can be blocked forever by arbitrary means is foolish. Neither legislative enactments that often are unconstitutional themselves nor public disorders that violate the spirit of law to which in other circumstances the resistance appeals, have done so or show any sign of being able to do so.

Such violence as has arisen rarely comes from Negroes. Their methods in the main have been those of the legal approach, the religious spirit, the petitions and protests that are guaranteed by the Bill of Rights, and demonstrations of personal dignity, calmness, courage, and forbearance: in all, the ways of civilized man. That they have impressed their fellow Americans and helped their cause is, I think, indisputable.

It is not here that the white South has anything to fear. Indeed, it is just here in this spirit that the white South can find fresh encouragement about the ultimate overcoming of the intellectual and cultural lag that seems to many people to present difficulties in schools and elsewhere. The subject needs firmer scientific basis than now exists. It includes some disturbing demonstrations, but American Negroes now can present enough striking personal achievements in enough aspects of American life to indicate the existence of a strong and broad potential of capacity. The handicaps of poverty and limited educational and economic opportunity may hang on for a long time, though they are clearly lessening. Meantime, the evidence mounts that modern Negro leadership possesses a sense of responsibility that the country associates with reasonable men.

The unmistakable fact is that, far from being stopped, the influences making for change grow larger and stronger rather than the other way around. The effect is that of a great river in which the current constantly increases because the sources of the current are continually renewed and enlarged. It cannot effectively be dammed. Its water would overflow or pour around any dam, and in time would burst the barrier. But intelligent engineering can facilitate the healthy flow of the river at the same time that it can guide and control it; and if these forces are in control the promise is immense energy for the common good and increased opportunity for all.

What, then, is the course of intelligence for the white people of the Southern States? Their problems and difficulties are large and numerous, and any road they take has perplexities. Law is no easier to enforce now than it has ever been in a region in which substantial proportions of the population oppose or doubt the wisdom or question the timing or have so many tough decisions to make that they try to make none at all. Old prejudices do not yield more readily in the South than anywhere else.

Yet there is another side to the equation, and though it is often ignored it is not the less important. For unpleasant though the prospect may seem to many Southerners, it possesses ruggedly practical elements which, if understood and grasped, can change the prospect. The opportunity, in a word, is immense.

Quite aside from the necessity that requires the decisions to be obeyed, the decisions when obeyed offer to the South the chance of dealing realistically and therefore in a new spirit with the greatest of its difficulties. There can be no mistake about what this is. The South can never rise to full stature in the nation, or witness the full development of its own people, and enjoy the results of that new applied energy, when a fourth of the population is so situated that it cannot contribute its full share to the life of the whole.

The presence of two races living side by side, one historically in secondary position and denied for centuries the opportunities of the other, affects Southern life at every point. The results are not measured in schools alone: they are measured in all aspects of life. Emotions, customs, habits, associations, and organizations, the manner of outward living and the shape of inward thinking, the statistics that record progress and accomplishment in government and society—all these are shaped and controlled by the dual-race basis of life. Industry, agriculture, and commerce; financial strength, wealth, and poverty; universities, libraries, museums, orchestras, and laboratories; costs in health, welfare, crime, and death; the geography of cities and towns; regional contentment with standards that produce "the best in the South" and ignore how far it may be below the best in the nation: all these too are organized, managed, sustained, or accepted in terms and because of the disparities of racial practices that fail to make the best of the two races.

Qualitatively the region drags its feet. Blessed by nature and rich in resources, it is hobbled by human failings which of itself the South has not yet been able to correct. Its white people lack larger opportunity because its black people lack even moderate opportunity. It is complacent with its weaknesses and long-suffering with a low level of excellence because its way of life makes it difficult under its racial handicaps to do better. It drives many of its youthful best away. They are less tolerant of the old ways, and they seek the peaks of accomplishment that the South's concentration on racial struggles denies. Public life, politics, and systems of government, and discussion, debate, maneuvers, and arrangements about all these, are managed and are carried out in terms quite different from those in other parts of the United States. Southern life has forced Southern thinking inward and away from American problems and toward sectional isolationism.

Does the modern South wish to continue this second-best sort of existence? I think not. It is being pulled back—against the will of many of its people at the moment—into the main stream of America. Now, all of a sudden, it has the opportunity of its life.

The forces that are running with the Supreme Court's decisions are powerful, and in the end they will prevail. The decisions themselves are expressing modern life, and in the end that life will prevail. The changes required have taken on the aura of judicial and constitutional dignity and respectability, and though this is still widely denied, and is broadly

resisted in the South, there is little doubt of what the final
result will be. Resistance crumbles steadily. It will crumble
increasingly and more swiftly.

But it still remains for the highest leadership of the Southern
States—as distinct for the most part from the political leadership—to assume command of the great transition and to make
of it something more than a long, bitter, and inevitably failing
rear-guard action. This is happening in specific ways in specific areas: Atlanta's schools, for one example. It has not
happened in the region as a whole. It has not happened
primarily because many of the wisest and most intelligent
men and women of the South have been pushed aside by the
organized opposition and by the political leaders who represent
that opposition. Only rarely has the natural leadership of mind
and spirit, that can rise above the opportunism of the hour,
stepped out in battle array—for that is what is necessary. If,
and when, this leadership goes into action, the impact will be
formidable and probably irresistible.

This is the obligation that rests today upon the educational
leaders of the colleges and universities, and of state and local
school departments, few of whom have exercised influence
thus far except as their silence has encouraged less intelligent,
but bolder, leadership to have its way. The transition manifests
itself conspicuously in the schools, and it is educational leadership that should be giving guidance and showing the way.

The responsibility rests upon the industrial, financial, and
commercial leaders from the world of business, whose power
with the public is immense. On occasion they have exercised
decisive influence, but the occasions have been few. Yet they
know that the economy of the South has never rested happily
on a racial basis and cannot possibly live healthily in the
modern world if there is lack of educational facilities, available

to all, that are excellent by national standards. Modern business demands, insists upon, and requires quality education.

The duty of influence rests upon organized religion, not only in the voices of its formal leaders and in its annual resolutions, many of which reflect a firm stand for the fundamentals, but also in its membership. Most of the members have turned away from their own leaders and simultaneously from principles to which in other circumstances they pledged allegiance.

The obligation, responsibility, and duty rest upon all men and women of good spirit and high intelligence who know the facts of life in the South but have hoped that the problems somehow would right themselves, and have waited for them to do so. They have waited in vain. The courts have been the activating agent, not any inherent Southern institution or corps of leadership. Yet the problems of the South require for their solution all possible wisdom and intelligence, all possible character, all possible statesmanship.

When this leadership does go into action, as it shows some signs of doing, its opportunity will be tremendous. For the historic transition that moves across the panorama before us today can lead to a clarification of Southern life and to an understanding of the relations of people in the South that go far beyond obedience to law. This is the opportunity to establish foundations for the sound growth of the human South, to its own happiness, and with fairness and justice for all. This is the opportunity to free the South from all crippling entanglements with its past that lessen its spiritual power in the land. Only thus can the South take its rightful place in the life of the nation and the world.

PRIDE AND PROTEST

Jonathan Daniels . . .

Editor of the *News and Observer*, Raleigh, N.C.; B.A. and M.A., University of North Carolina; reporter in Louisville and Raleigh; Washington correspondent for the *News and Observer*, 1925-28; member of *Fortune Magazine* staff; assistant director, Office of Civilian Defense, 1942; administrative assistant to President Roosevelt, 1943-45; press secretary to President Truman, 1945; Democratic national committeeman from North Carolina, 1949-52; became editor of *News and Observer* in 1948, on the death of his father, Josephus Daniels; has served as U.S. representative on the U.N. Commission on Prevention of Discrimination and Protection of Minorities, Public Advisory Board of the Economic Cooperation Administration and Mutual Security Agency, and the Federal Hospital Council of the Public Health Service; member of the U.S. Advisory Commission on Information; author of *Clash of Angels* (a novel that brought him a Guggenheim Fellowship for study in Europe); *A Southerner Discovers the South; A Southerner Discovers New England; Tar Heels: A Portrait of North Carolina; Frontier on the Potomac; The Man of Independence; The End of Innocence; Prince of Carpetbaggers; Forrest is the Future;* and for young people: *Mosby, Gray Ghost of the Confederacy; Stonewall Jackson;* and *Robert E. Lee.*

Many of us, when we were young and shared the adventure in speed largely provided then by railroad trains, liked to count the telegraph poles as we sped by them. They represented distance even if they did not certainly point directions.

We need more often to count the markers of our change now. There are plenty of politicians to tell Southerners in this period of jet change that the South is going nowhere in altering its customs. The truth, of course, is that there is no greater Southern illusion. The markers of Dixie's resistance, massive or diminutive, are falling behind at an accelerated rate. In a period that has pierced the universe, nothing is so impotent as Southern stubbornness in a changing world. Nobody will stop the change. Nobody could if he wished to. And the secret truth is that the South is far readier for revolution than reaction.

Nearly a quarter of a century ago now, when I traveled the South trying to describe it, I first thought of naming a book I wrote, "Eat, Mule, Eat the Azaleas." I am not sure now exactly what that meant. A professor who borrowed it for a chapter heading for a volume he wrote said he knew precisely what it meant. There were plently of mules then on a Southern land occupied by more people than it could feed. There were plenty of azaleas, too—already shown in gorgeous gardens, for a price. Fortunately there are even more azaleas now. Sadly, we cannot say the same about the mule. The problem, now as then, is the man who once was behind him.

And fortunately, despite continuing need, in comparison with past poverty and past appearances, the condition of people below the Potomac seems now like Christmas in the slave quarters. The late Confederacy counts its cars and complains about the parking. Sometimes the width of its new highways seems to do a better job of crop control than the government. Oak Ridge and Aiken have been added to TVA. More and more factories have been coming with more and more jobs, and governors are out frantically chasing more, not only North but overseas.

In the South, towns have grown at a greater rate than elsewhere; so have the number of machines on our land. And, to state a more startling if grisly statistic, in the quarter-century from 1909 to 1934, nearly a thousand Negroes were lynched: an average of forty a year. In the last quarter-century the total has been fewer than a hundred—fewer in all those twenty-five years than in the single year of 1900, at the beginning of our century. Discrimination remains but the halter is being put upon its hoodlum defenders.

The Southern States have reasons for pride. Their colleges have grown almost in geometric progression and they still look apprehensively at the mounting probabilities of young people seeking admission. The schools for Negroes have been miraculously improved—perhaps under an outside prod, but in magnificent native progress, nevertheless. Yet it cannot be denied that in the same period some Southern states have put on their books laws that provide for the closing of the schools under certain conditions.

This is, of course, a plan which, if any State dared to apply it, would not be secession from the Union but secession from civilization. Clearly, however, the South's progress in education and other things in recent years has not merely been from Eugene Talmadge to Orval Faubus. We have come forward from the great lament Margaret Mitchell wrote in *Gone with the Wind*. It may well be that the South's present mood was described by a man from Columbus, Mississippi, in the title of his play, *Cat on a Hot Tin Roof*.

Only the half-blind elsewhere see only a stubborn single-minded South. It never has existed and does not exist now. Undoubtedly, many Southerners have dodged their dilemma as they have talked and written steadily about its two main and often monotonous subjects: industrialization and integration. Many have indulged themselves to the full in those supposedly Southern characteristic postures, pride and protest. But more Southerners than those who make the angry headlines know that the South was a region of philosophers once—perhaps briefly, but greatly—and a region that shaped American ideas about liberty and democracy. There is native consciousness of lapse in both, early and late. Also there is an increasing feeling that the South has recently been getting too little intellectual and spiritual nutriment from its politicians who once, long ago, were its philosophers, too.

Uneasily Southerners begin to see that the great, significant thing that has happened to the South is that behind recent leaders, the region—not the Negroes in it but the region itself—has somehow lost its understanding of its place and that in the strategy of history such supposed leaders have lost all contact with the meaning of power. Indeed, sometimes under the oratory of some of its poorest substitutes for statesmen the South seems an emotional area that became more arrogant as its impotence increased.

Suspicion of this development grows in the increasing recognition that the task of the South is to grow again in greatness as it hopes desperately to grow in wealth. And that task becomes more difficult every day despite the unveiling of new factories. It is impossible of attainment in terms of the South described by its most belligerent politicians. Such men will not even face the fact of greatest significance in Dixie. It is that the meek have inherited the earth. Or, to say it otherwise, the lemmings have taken command. Their flight is not to death. What has happened is that those who have been ejected are the unsuspected masters in the Southern house. In America the

Negroes have greater political power than the Southern politicians. And in the South the mob has begun to disintegrate behind the discriminators.

It should be unnecessary to point the mechanization of farms, the dispersal of people, the urbanization and the migration that have taken place in the Southern States in the last twenty-five years. Perhaps the whole process began long ago when the boll weevil arrived as an enemy alien. Within those years such a great cotton farmer as the late Oscar Johnson of the huge Delta and Pine plantations in Mississippi expressed his fixed doubts about the usefuless of the mechanical cotton picker and his preference for the old plantation economy and its social and economic patterns. Others still prefer it. But the clear fact to every traveler in the South today is the increasing disappearance of the mule. The man who trudged behind him is disappearing, too. The most important fact in the years behind us is the movement of the Negroes. That has changed our towns and our countrysides. And the equivalent of the Underground Railroad in our times has been pulled in broad daylight by diesel engines.

Much of that movement and change has been sheer gain for the South. Many white Southerners regard the movement of the Negro as good riddance, particularly when it is northward. And in important respects the change has been gain for whites and Negroes together. When I first rode about the South as inquisitive reporter in 1937, more people were trying to live on less land—and a more worn land—than was under cultivation at the time of the Civil War. I don't need to point the change to you. The barrens and the old fields are green today. Pines for paper grow beyond the teaching of Dr. Charles Holmes Herty, who labored as a chemist in Georgia as this quarter-century began. The tended forests have spread, even though recalcitrant and reluctant Southerners set more arson fires in the woods than any other people in America.

But the great change, as you know, has been on the cultivated lands. And it has come fast. I quote some figures from Eugene Butler, of Dallas, president of *The Progressive Farmer:* "In 1940, the South harvested 103 million acres in crops. In 1958, the acreage fell to $86\frac{1}{2}$ million. Meanwhile, since 1930, pastures of all kinds have climbed from 152 million acres to 222 million acres—about 75 per cent; the number of cattle is up 130 per cent." Contemplating those figures, Southerners may be contented as the cows. But Mr. Butler said: "Between 1940 and 1958, the South cut cotton production by ten million acres. . . ." And he added significantly, ". . . with these lost acres went five million people."

And the central problem of the South is where they went.

To town, of course. And in a multitude of Southern towns that process has stirred chamber-of-commerce pride. Even in Southern town and city, however, that process has not been altogether simple. It underlies the almost panting Southern pursuit of industry today. But we must, in pride over the pace of Southern industrial development, still realize that one of the chief things the South has to sell industry is labor supply, and that the availability of this commodity is another name for the continuing underemployment of men and women living in the South. The movement to the cities creates another situation, one emphasized and illustrated by the fact that today in Richmond, the old capital of the Confederacy, there are more Negro than white children in the city's schools —and there may be more Negro adults and voters, too, before long.

But even Richmond and the other Southern cities are only stops on the line. In 1960 ten million persons born in the

South were living in other regions. That figure is increasing
still. But even that figure is more than equal to what would
have happened if all the people in Mississippi, Louisiana, South
Carolina, and Arkansas had moved away—more than equal
to what would have happened if everybody in the two Southern states most populous in 1950, North Carolina and Georgia,
had packed up and lit out. Fortunately, some other people, not
generally regarded as carpetbaggers, have come South. And
the swap, man for man, may have been a bargain for the
South. But customers are gone. Citizens are lost. And the
South's place in the nation has been reduced.

And it was while this migration and emigration proceeded
at an accelerated rate that the event occurred which the South
dates as almost as significant as the firing on Fort Sumter—
perhaps as Lee's surrender at Appomattox. On May 17, 1954,
the U.S. Supreme Court announced its decision in the case of
Brown vs. Board of Education.

It is still with us. Since then, several Southern states have
passed laws providing for the closing of their schools if this
decision is enforced. The governor of another state assumed
that power. The doctrine of Massive Resistance was announced, even if it was not quite adequately devised to avoid
rebuke. And it seems an understatement to say that more of the
thinking of those who make a craft, if not an art, of politics
has been devoted to this subject than any other in the years
since the decision was rendered. In some states defiance of the
law seemed to become the minimum requirement of politicians,
and the maximum fulfillment of that role appeared to be the
best assurance of office.

That may have been necessary for politicians. But the political facts as well as the politicians deserve a consideration that
they have not been sufficiently given. The South is always a re-

gion difficult to define. The census South is not the South always described by the social scientists. We have the confusion of the Southern Governor's Conference, which recently was attended by the Governor of Delaware, but not by the Governor of Texas, who had transferred his conferring to the West. Perhaps in terms of present emotions and present problems, the South, as an angry word in the American language, may best be identified as those Southern states which passed laws providing for the closing of their schools in the event of integration. They run from the Potomac to the Gulf. More significantly as a block, they are states from which people have run—or moved—away. And with the departure of people they have significantly lost votes in the Congress and the Electoral College.

The be-damned-if-we-do Southern States are not the only states that are highly emotional politically about what we call the Southern problem. There is an increasing number of Northern states that have Negro populations in excess of half a million. In these states the Negroes constitute a solid, block-voting balance of power in elections. I was in New York during a recent campaign, and I can testify that no Southern politician ever damned the NAACP with more enthusistic violence than Northern politicians of both parties put into the wooing of the Negro vote.

Such states have more—and increasingly more—votes in the Congress and in the Electoral College. And other Northern and Western states are more apt to stand with them than with the hard core states of the late Confederacy. A South that survived the higher mathematics of the interest piled up on the charge accounts of the time merchants should understand the plain arithmetic of political power.

It is not necessary that Southerners like this situation. It is essential to good sense at home that they recognize it. And what they need to recognize is that as Southern angers have grown, the South, in terms of regional power in the national life, has lost even its second place to the West. The West, on issues dear to the South, is aligned with the North. The obvious answer to that is not some impotent gestures in neo-secession of one kind or another, but a statesmanship equal to the best in the Southern past. Such statesmanship may be hard to find. Too often in our history it has been disregarded. But the cry of neo-secession, which so often seems to come now as before from South Carolina, is not only futile but comic. This time the nation wouldn't have to resupply Fort Sumter. Supplies would be short in Charleston if the United States closed the U.S. Navy Yard.

So the last quarter-century ended not merely with the shaping of the angry problem of integration at the time of the South's highest hope of industrialization. It ended at a time when the South seemed to grow richer as it grew weaker. And also at a time when, despite all Southern gains, Southerners are sometimes almost desperately aware of their needs: it is still the poorest section despite all development, as it is still the most ignorant section despite all sacrifices for education. Factories have risen in these years, and already, too, the walls of resistance have been falling. A governor who pressed for a system under which schools might be closed entertained the black president of an African republic at a dinner for ladies and gentlemen of both colors in the banquet room of the first state university to open its doors in the South. Indeed, this governor's act was a realistic recognition that the South in this nation cannot disregard the problems of the surrounding and stirring world.

It is still not certain that Dixie can move as it should move without an explosion in the last years of our century. I suspect that explosion is a fundamental aspect of the Southern— and also the American—character. It is our virtue that we do not abandon our faith or our opinions with docility. Change is painful. And change can be dangerous. Still, I believe that a quarter-century in the South that has been so much concerned with industrialization and integration must produce in the next quarter-century a statesmanship that can put the two together with the most creativeness and the least pain.

What happened to us with the dispersal of the people from the land was not merely a lemming-like movement of peoples to a deadly complex of insoluble problems. The period behind us has been marked by the escape of the South from the rusted chains that lingered from slavery, and it was an escape of white and colored people together.

Southerners lived—and often in a content that seems lost today—in a land where the presence of a habituated, ignorant, politically impotent, rural people, who would work for a pittance, made new techniques and new machines seem senseless in a plantation economy. It seemed beside the point that so many poor people kept the whole region poor, too. Maybe opportunities elsewhere for them pulled people away before machines on the land pushed them.

The fact is that the South has got out of old ruts. And in the process has made a river. It can be as frightening as flood. It could drain a great region of its people and their powers. And that drain will not stop until the South is developed in generous terms for all its people. Those who said long ago that to educate a "nigger" would only ruin a good field hand may have been exactly right by their own lights and their own desires. By their judgment certainly many of the colored people are ruined now. In the same process a lot of "crackers" were ruined along Tobacco Road, too. People have lost their roots. Discontent moves more people than gasoline. And hungers have mounted from pot liquor to power boats. It is probably not all gain that the drag race has taken the place of the coon hunt.

But in history we do not deal with romantic details we would prefer. We must face the realistic facts that we find. A fact that we cannot escape at the end of this quarter-century is that the Negro is no longer content in his place—the place that the South designed for him; and, more important, that he is able to get out of it even if his choice of a city slum over a country cabin seems hardly a wise one to many.

But note carefully, the once-called "poor whites" are not content in their old, fixed status either. Some in sullenness only burn the tended forests that were once ranging grounds of their scrub cattle. But more are made indistinguishable from their "betters" by beauty parlors and chain-store clothes.

I believe that industrial development will produce the jobs that young white men and women need in the South. Also, I make bold to say that we cannot safely for ourselves continue the process by which the best brains in the colored race, to make a decent living, must be teachers, while whites can get jobs and make money with less education. Long continued, that really would be the business of putting the bottom rail on top intellectually. Already job discrimination has in some parts of the South reversed the pattern of slavery: the white folks work to keep the colored folks in idleness on relief. Not the Negro's threat, but the Negro's need must be our greatest concern.

As one Southerner, I want to live in a South which can keep its people for the development of a long-loved and well-loved region. And keep them on standards worthy of the best aspirations of Americans. They want to stay. The dispersal of Southerners, the great flow of migration, is hardly less significant to sensitive observers in the South than the regular, crowded, recurrent, homesick movement southward, too. Sometimes I think the South is most loved by those who leave it, but cannot always happily stay away.

The Suwannee song is not lost in Southern hearts today. The problem of statesmanship is to keep more who love it from leaving. The North and West were built by the arrival, not the departure, of all kinds of people. And some of those who came found contempt and antagonism here as well as opportunity. The South will not long flourish if it gains plants and loses people. And it will not be the South if it does not hope to keep all its people at decent standards and in good, warm relationships. Such relationships are not impossible, though their arrangement in new times may be difficult. But the one impossible idiot in the South is the politician—and those who listen to him, too—who at full cry goes hunting for the new carpetbaggers while insisting that there must be no reconstruction in terms of new ideas at home. That did not happen before. It will not happen now. But a South which recognizes its responsibility at home for all its people need not fear that recurrence of overwrought legends of reconstruction awaits it. It may indeed learn in surprise that the problems to which it gives priority are less serious than they seem.

The past twenty-five years in the South have been the quarter-century of Southern escape. That can be best understood in recognition that the Southern movement has been a part of revolution in the whole world. The notion that hunger was inescapable has passed. Immobility is no longer regarded as morality. The least peoples have somehow gained a sense of their own part in the possibilities of our age. It is, of course, not true that Russia rushed forward from the sickle to the sputnik in half a century. But the change in the South has included the movement from cotton to Cape Canaveral. It is true that everywhere gain and loss have been intermingled, and anger and eagerness, too. Those who surge forward in hope may sink back under the new tyranny of others or the equal tyranny of obsolete thinking, obsolete listening, and defunct but still defiant politicians.

The recent past has been the era of massive change, not massive resistance. The hope for all that is left of this century in the South is that change be recognized as the basis for thinking, not sulking. What is required is not a new New South (that is already here) but a Southern statesmanship, backed by courageous citizenship, which, without repudiating its place in the nation and the world, will still put old need and new hope together to keep the South, white and black, at home, with equal opportunity and dignity for all.

MEANWHILE, IN MISSISSIPPI— SOLIDARITY FOREVER?

Hodding Carter III . . .

Managing editor of *The Delta Democrat-Times*, Greenville, Miss.; native of New Orleans; graduate of Greenville, Miss., High School and Princeton University (*summa cum laude*) in Woodrow Wilson School of Public and International Affairs (winner of school prize for his senior thesis); joined Marines, released as first lieutenant in 1959; worked as cub reporter on old New Orleans *Item*, joined staff of *Democrat-Times* in 1959; won Sigma Delta Chi award for editorial writing for 1960; author of *The South Strikes Back*, about the Mississippi White Citizens' Council.

The roll-call of Southern communities that have begun at least token public-school integration in response to Federal court prodding was significantly lengthened in the fall of 1961 with the peaceful desegregation of schools in Dallas, Memphis, and Atlanta. In the last two cities, massive resistance on the secondary school level in the Deep South was shattered for the first time. While the number of children involved was not impressive, the psychological effect on the rest of the Black Belt South was immense.

But one state, which shares with Alabama and South Carolina the distinction of maintaining total segregation at all levels in the public schools, shows no signs of yielding to a process most white Southerners have grudgingly begun to accept as inevitable. The state is Mississippi. After almost eight years of mounting pressure, it is still virtually impossible to find any public manifestations of the fatalism that many whites are privately expressing.

As the pressure has intensified, in fact, Mississippi resistance has tended to stiffen rather than crumble. It is the one Southern state which showed a completely unified front in defying the new Interstate Commerce Commission ruling on the desegregation of interstate facilities. State laws were invoked in every city to preserve segregation in the local waiting rooms and terminal restaurants. A Federal Court struck down segregation in two terminals, but in one an attempt by Negroes to use the white facilities brought vicious rioting and in the other there were no known attempts at integration by early 1962.

The observer therefore would be hard pressed to find a major chink in Mississippi's segregationist forces. There is a handful of white dissidents, and there is a growing number of Negro militants, but neither is formed into a strength that can wield any great influence. Support for the continuation of segregation in Mississippi is pervasive, sometimes subtle and immensely strong. To a high degree it is vested in the Citizens' Council.

It is difficult to explain to an outsider just how powerful a force this white-supremacy group has become. Perhaps the hardest point to grasp is that the Citizens' Council in Mississippi —no matter how dubious its aims, repugnant its methods or despicable its philosophy—is not made up of hooded figures meeting furtively in back alleys.

Its leadership is drawn not from the pool hall but from the country club. Its membership generally exhibits the attitudes of the middle and upper classes rather than of the poor white. And its aims are not couched in violent language but in the careful embroidery of states' rights and constitutionalism.

In fact, when the first Council was formed eight years ago by a group of community leaders in the Delta town of Indianola, one central purpose was to retain control of resistance to desegreation in the hands of the "better people." Then, it was a semisecret society. Today, membership in the Citizens' Council has come to be akin to membership in the Rotary or Lions Club. It is such an accepted mark of distinction, in fact, that many candidates for public or organizational office carefully add their participation in the Council to their listings of civic enterprises in which they have engaged.

The Council's control of the state was made formal in August, 1959. In that month, Ross Barnett—against the opposition of Mississippi's two living ex-Governors and all but one of the state's daily newspapers, but with the all-out support of the Council—won a landslide victory in the Democratic primary runoff for Governor.

Since then, the Council has all but completed the construction of a political machine whose power is publicly unchallenged by any major state official. One of its dramatic accomplishments was the narrow victory scored in November, 1960, by a slate of Presidential "free electors" who eventually cast the state's eight Electoral College votes for Senator Harry F. Byrd of Virginia.

Far more important to the Council's purposes, however, and better illustrative of its grip on the state government, was the decision by the State Sovereignty Commission in late 1960 to donate $5,000 a month from state tax money to support the

Council's radio and television program, Citizens' Council Forum. The members of the commission, formed by the Legislature in 1956 "to protect the sovereignty of the state of Mississippi," include the Governor, and are nearly to a man Council members.

The grant, combined with a lump-sum donation of $20,000, had brought the Council over $100,000 from the public treasury by 1962. Although an internal power struggle in the Sovereignty Commission resulted in a $500-a-month cut in the donation, no one seriously believes the commission will eliminate it altogether in the near future.

There are many other examples of the Council's influence in the state government. Perhaps most significant is the fact that William Simmons, editor of the Council's newspaper and administrator of the state Council association, has become a constant companion of Governor Barnett, traveling with him when he makes out-of-state talks (many of which Simmons reputedly writes) and sitting in as an "observer" at most meetings of the Sovereignty Commission.

During the regular session of the legislature in 1960, that body acted as little more than a rubber stamp for bills that had Council endorsement. One gave local congregations the right to secede from their parent churches, taking church property with them, if they found themselves in conflict with the national denominations' doctrines. It was passed despite claims that it violated the constitutional separation of church and state. And many of Governor Barnett's major appointments were of men who were on the Council's state board of directors.

Individual Councils vary from town to town, but the general pattern is much the same. One may screen new members more rigorously than another; some are relatively inactive. Most hold annual membership drives during which they make heavy use of newspaper advertising. One Council advertised that a prospective member need merely "walk into the bank." In another town, a membership application could be filled out at the local hotel. In countless restaurants across the state, Citizens' Council literature can be picked up with the tooth-picks at the cashier's counter.

The local organization's president is invariably a prominent citizen, and the board of directors is drawn largely from the community's Who's Who. When meetings are held, which isn't often, the same rough form of Robert's Rules of Order followed in most civic clubs is observed. The chairman begins by calling on a minister—most often a Baptist—for a prayer. Committee reports, if any, are heard, and the main business of the evening follows.

As often as not, the meeting will be open to the public, and will feature a main speaker and several lesser lights. The fea-tured attraction inevitably urges continued adherence to segre-gation and states' rights, lashes the Supreme Court, the National Association for the Advancement of Colored People, church groups, "liberals" and "moderates," and invariably ends with a call for a united front of dues-paying members to stem the tide of change.

At a closed meeting, the main order of business may be any-thing from a discussion of the difficulties of collecting dues to the formulation of a plan to deal with a local white or Negro "trouble-maker." One or two hotheads will jump up and let loose with impassioned speeches calling for radical and im-mediate action—usually a midnight call on the offender. The conservatives then will make themselves heard, calm down the firebrands, and smother the proposal, although they may then enforce an approach that will accomplish the same ends by more indirect means.

As a result of the perpetuation of conservative control, no act of racial violence in Mississippi has ever been directly connected to the Citizens' Council. Those incidents that have occurred may be indirectly traceable to the climate engendered by the Council, but it is a theoretical relationship. The Council has found it doesn't need to operate in that way to get results.

Initially, the use of economic pressure against dissenting whites and Negroes was the main weapon, and to some extent it is still used, particularly against Negroes. But as the Council has developed it has found that the isolation of moderate and liberal whites from the rest of the white community and the complete destruction of interracial communication are infinitely more productive and far easier to accomplish.

To a degree that is hard to convey to someone who does not live in Mississippi, the Citizens' Council has managed to divert the antipathy of most white Mississippians for integration into a mold that includes the total rejection of any deviation from the *status quo*. Blind adherence to "our way of life" is the unending refrain of the Citizens' Council's newspapers, its leaders and most of its estimated 80,000 members (a figure claimed by Council leaders and impossible to check). Since this slogan touches a theme that has been central to Mississippi history since the Civil War, the approach is highly successful.

There are numerous examples of the price demanded for failure to walk in the Council-enforced lockstep. Several years ago, a minister chose to defend two white men accused of being "integrationists" at a Citizens' Council-inspired mass meeting held to demand that they leave the county. Within a few months, the pastor was deprived of his church by the unanimous vote of its governing board. Other ministers across the state got the message.

In the same county, the woman editor of a small weekly has battled the Council since the day it was organized. When a whispering campaign and advertising boycott failed to drive her out of business, a group of Citizens' Council leaders started another newspaper. She has managed to survive, thanks almost entirely to her own gutty determination not to go under, but again the point was made and duly noted by other newspaper men tempted to oppose the Council.

The primary technique of isolation is simply a variation of the big lie. Those who don't go along with the Council are tarred over and over, in public and private, with the same old phrases that most Southerners still dread. The dissenter is a "nigger lover," a "scalawag," an "integrationist," or a "renegade white." When the charges are repeated often enough in Mississippi's present climate of opinion, they begin to stick, and the nonconformist becomes the local pariah.

Lately, a new weapon has been added to the Council's arsenal. Professional anti-Communists have been brought into the state, usually under the auspices of the Sovereignty Commission, and while they deal chiefly with the alleged Communist penetration of every facet of American life, they earn their fee in Mississippi by implying that those who challenge the segregationist line are members of the Communist apparatus. This, too, has been effective in neutralizing the Council's opponents, for Mississippians are no less prone to see a Communist behind every demand for change than are many of their fellow Americans.

After Memphis and Atlanta and Dallas, the Council is stronger than ever in Mississippi. Paradoxically, it has been reinvigorated as the struggle has moved closer to the state. And certain events within the state, although they will lead in the long run to the destruction of the cause the Council supports, also have had the effect of giving the Council an immediate shot in the arm.

In the last half of 1961, Mississippi experienced for the first time sit-ins, voter registration drives, Freedom Riders, Federal vote suits, and court action for the desegregation of the state university. The Council hastened to capitalize on each.

Nothing, however, was as much of a godsend to the Council as the continued forays of the Freedom Riders. Even while their exploits were focusing national attention on segregation in interstate facilities in the South, Council leaders were singling out the "friction riders" as a convenient symbol of "outside interference." The success with which officials in the capital city of Jackson kept the segregation lid on while maintaining law and order as hundreds of Freedom Riders poured into the city was made-to-order propaganda for the Council, which has always promised that segregation could be preserved without violence. The violence in McComb was exploited as the inevitable result of too much pushing and as proof of the necessity for segregation to preserve order.

From the moment it was clear that the first Freedom Riders were coming to Mississippi after their violence-packed journey through Alabama, the Council took the lead in urging public order, while its spokesmen poured out a steady stream of vituperation upon the organizations and individuals connected with the group. As each new busload arrived in Jackson, Council membership efforts intensified and, if its leaders are to be believed, Council membership grew.

The same was true in south Mississippi after Negro registration attempts resulted in beatings in mid-1961. In counties where the Council had been either dormant or nonexistent, new units sprang up overnight. Revitalization was reported in other areas where there were no incidents, but where Council leaders spurred organization or activation as a means of preventing Negro civil-rights activity.

Through it all, the simple, single Council line has been: If we will only organize, maintain our solidarity and fight the good fight, we can still win.

Robert Patterson, a Delta planter who was one of the founders and is now secretary of the Citizens' Council, sounded the call for all Council supporters after Memphis desegregated. In a letter to the editor of a Memphis newspaper, Patterson wrote:

"To be subjected to integration is one thing, but to submit to it is quite another. If we are subjected to it, we can resist it, contain it and eventually expel it, but if we submit to it and accept it, in my opinion the destruction is likely to be permanent and irrevocable."

The Council is infinitely strengthened in Mississippi by the fact that the state is still basically agrarian, made up of small communities and towns in which the dissenter can find few allies. There is no large metropolitan center here, no Memphis or New Orleans or Atlanta. The largest city is Jackson (population 145,000), and there the Council has been most successful at organizing. The city's three dailies either echo the Council's beliefs or remain silent, with the exception of the *Jackson State-Times*, whose editor on occasions takes stands at direct variance with the Council's. It is almost impossible to find a business or professional man who is not at least a nominal Council member. It just isn't good business not to belong.

None of this is to say that as the reverses mount, as the Federal courts strike down one after another of the state's segregation laws, the Council will be able to stem the tide. It has not been able to do so elsewhere and will not be able to here. What this does mean, however, is that in Mississippi as in no other state there will be continued fierce resistance long after the first battle is lost. And in Mississippi, the final alternative, a statewide school closing in the face of a desegregation decree, is the one most likely to be used.

There is opposition to the Citizens' Council in Mississippi, and the total conformity it would like is still far from realized. But the white opposition for the most part has been belated, isolated, and ineffective. Every time there has been a chance that internal opposition might coalesce, events, usually originating from outside the state, have diverted public attention and exerted strong pressure for white solidarity—as in the case of the Freedom Riders. If the Council was one of the chief beneficiaries in Mississippi of their efforts, the moderates were the chief losers.

Perhaps the best chance the Council's opponents had for an issue around which they could rally involved Billy Barton, a University of Mississippi undergraduate, and native of the state, who disclosed in the spring of 1961 that the Sovereignty Commission had built up a secret dossier on his private life which contained a number of lies and innuendoes about his alleged role in the "integrationist apparatus," most of them supplied by a high Citizens' Council source. Barton charged that the misinformation was being used by state officials in an attempt to insure his defeat in the campus election for editor of the university newspaper.

Most Mississippians were shocked by the Barton case, which carried with it the obvious implication that other files were being compiled by the commission's agents in a manner reminiscent of a police state. But the combination of time, Barton's defeat in the election (ironically enough by an opponent who was considered more "liberal" on the race issue), and the advent of the Freedom Riders were sufficient to blur the issue. Since then other instances of secret police work by commission agents have been revealed, but their impact has been blunted by the battle over segregation being fought on other fronts.

The spurt of civil rights activity has had one positive effect, of course. The Negro community, which makes up almost half the state's population, is far more militant as a result of the events of the past year.

Yet it is just this spirit, when it is publicly expressed by words or deeds, which feeds the Council's mill. Here, at home, is the very threat its spokesmen have been warning of for seven years. White Mississippians may be unable to see the obvious point that the process of change had reached the state despite the Council, but they are quick to embrace any group which promises a reversal of the trend. This promise the Council supplies.

There are several reasonable conjectures about what the future holds. There can be little doubt that the Citizens' Council in Mississippi is going to get stronger before it gets weaker. The peak of the crisis has not been reached, and the Council feeds on crisis. Already it is marshaling its forces to support the closing of the schools when the inevitable court decree is handed down.

Whether it can rally as wide support once the defeats begin to register is doubtful, and if violence develops on a large scale the Council is sure to lose many of its supporters from the upper economic and social strata. But with tradition behind it, and with the political influence it now has, only the most optimistic could contend that the Citizens' Council will not be a potent force in Mississippi in the foreseeable future.

BUT IN FLORIDA—
WE CANNOT
WASH OUR HANDS . . .

LeRoy Collins . . .

Governor of Florida 1955-61; now president of the National Association of Broadcasters; native of Tallahassee, Fla.; attorney; Leon County representative in the Florida Legislature, 1934-40; member of the Florida Senate, 1940-54; naval lieutenant during Second World War; former chairman of the Southern Regional Education Board; former chairman of the Southern Governors' Conference and of the National Governors' Conference; member of the National Advisory Committee for the Peace Corps; chairman of the Department of Commerce Area Redevelopment Authority Advisory Committee.

From among several suggestions made by Governor Collins for his article in this book, I selected the transcript of a radio and television speech he made while governor of Florida, to his constituents throughout the State, when it appeared that Florida might be headed for a social explosion unless someone could inject a calming sanity into the situation. The controversy was an outgrowth of sit-in demonstrations of the sort conducted at lunch counters in many parts of the South. The first sit-in was held by four Negro students from A. and T. College in Greensboro, N.C., on Feb. 1, 1960. From there the sit-ins spread—eventually to Tallahassee, Governor Collins's home town and the state capital, a small city in the tier of rural counties stretching across North Florida, along the Georgia and Alabama lines.

There, on a Saturday afternoon in the early spring of 1960, a group of students from Florida A. and M. University (Negro) and Florida State University (white) who were members of the Congress of Racial Equality requested service at the lunch counter in a variety store. The management of the store did not ask them to leave, but closed the counter for the rest of the day. The next Saturday CORE students attempted another sit-in demonstration there, and again the managers of the store did not ask them to leave. Now occurred an indication of what was to come: city officials and business leaders in Tallahassee took a "hard line" of resistance to any desegregation of lunch counters, despite the efforts of Governor Collins to achieve moderation. The mayor of the town appeared at the store and ordered the students to leave. When they refused, they were arrested under a municipal ordinance empowering the mayor to prohibit any assembly that might tend to cause public turbulence and disorder. They were not arrested under a state law that says a merchant has the right to select his customers.

On the third Saturday, the students returned to the lunch counters. Still the managers of the store did not ask them to leave. A group of white men, led by a soda jerk, appeared with toy baseball bats. The police, again at the mayor's direction, arrested the sit-in demonstrators but made no move against the whites. Outraged by what they felt was official partiality, some 100 A. and M. students marched into the center of town. In the central park they encountered a large group of hostile whites. The two groups neared each other; they stood face to face, two feet apart; then a Negro girl leading the students turned them back to the campus. Now an even larger group of A. and M. students formed on the campus and started to march uptown, in two columns. They were turned back this time by city police and state highway patrolmen. Tear gas was used against one of the columns.

What would happen on the fourth Saturday? Extensive news reports carried inflammatory statements made by some members of the state legislature and by extremist leaders. There were rumors that a bus-load of Negro agitators from out of the state was assembling on the A. and M. campus armed with baseball bats and prepared to invade the downtown area (in his broadcast Governor Collins revealed the absurdity of this report). Local merchants began hiding shotguns and pistols behind their counters. The fever spread. The students of Negro high schools and private Negro colleges had begun sit-in demonstrations in Tampa, St. Augustine, and other cities. The sit-in was becoming a major issue in the current gubernatorial campaign. Several candidates telegraphed congratulations to Tallahassee officials for their stand and their action.

Meanwhile, Governor Collins's efforts to calm his troubled state, with appeals for respect for law and order, were apparently fruitless. His statements were given inflammatory and distorted treatment in the Tallahassee press and in wire reports originating there—at one point a misquotation distributed by the Associated Press stated that he had said the sit-ins were Communist-inspired. This was entirely out of character, but the garbled statement was used by David Lawrence as the basis for a newspaper column that received national distribution. As a consequence of this press treatment, the Negroes began to lose confidence in the fairness of the governor, and the more militant among them were becoming increasingly influential.

The chasm between the Negroes and the whites deepened and widened.

At this point, Governor Collins arranged the first state-wide radio and television network in the state's history, to appeal directly to the citizens in a heart-to-heart talk during the quiet of a Sunday afternoon. When the governor's plan became known, moderate Negro leaders were able to dissuade A. and M. students from conducting the demonstrations that they had planned for Saturday, March 19, in Tallahassee. Governor Collins appeared the next day without text, though with a sketchy outline of notes. This is what he said, edited to eliminate only certain minor, irrelevant comments.—H.N.

I want to thank station WFGA and all the other broadcasting stations throughout the state for giving me this opportunity of coming into your living room this afternoon and talking to you about some problems about which I am very gravely concerned and that affect every man, woman and child in our state. . . .

I want to talk to you about race relations. I had a group of my friends come over to see me yesterday and they said very frankly, "Governor, we don't think you should make this broadcast you are talking about tomorrow afternoon." I asked why and they said, "Well, you have less than a year now to serve in this office and certainly you know that whatever you say is going to make some people mad, and we just don't see the reason why you should stick your neck out or become involved in a discussion of that very explosive issue."

Well, I don't follow that sort of logic. I believe this is a very grave and serious matter facing the people of this state, affecting all of us, and I think the people of this state expect their governor to have convictions, and I think the people of this state when their governor has convictions about a matter expect him to express those convictions directly to them.

That's the policy I've been following as your governor. I know many times that I have taken stands that many people have not approved of. But I still believe that I have the respect of the people of Florida because I believe those people have felt I was sincere in my position and I think by and large where they have differed with me, they have come later to feel that there was considerable logic in the stand that I took in respect to them.

Now let me say this: I believe very deeply that I represent every man, woman, and child in this state as their governor, whether that person is black or white, whether that person is rich or poor, or whether that person is influential or not influential.

A governor, if he is worth his salt, has a deep responsibility for all the people and I feel that responsibility. I want to say this to you, too, that I am not a candidate for anything. It seems almost every time I speak out about anything these days and for some time past now, I am projected as being a candidate for vice president or having some personal motives of some sort. Now that is absolutely—there is nothing to that.

I believe that the face of Florida—the image of Florida—is not in its pine trees or in its palm trees or even in its orange trees, but in the people of this state. I believe that large star on our map of the United States that represents Florida stands for the people of Florida.

Now let me review briefly something of the history of this racial strife that we are contending with. It was on last February 1 that four Negro college students from a North Carolina college went into a Woolworth store in Greensboro, N.C. They bought some tooth paste and other minor items at one of the counters, then turned over to the lunch counter and ordered a cup of coffee. The waitress there said, "I'm sorry, we do not serve colored people here." One of the students said, "Why, I have just been served here. I bought a tube of tooth paste over there." She said, "Well, we serve you over there, but we do not serve you here."

That was the first of these demonstrations. Many followed there in Greensboro involving hundreds of people. They spread throughout North Carolina, on to Virginia, to South Carolina, to all of the other states of the South, including Florida.

And we have had many throughout our state and, unlike some people assume, not all of these demonstrations were sponsored by students; in fact, only a minority have been sponsored by students. But the worst of all, of course, has occurred, I think, as some of you know, in Tallahassee. And there it was largely sponsored by students from the Florida A. & M. University, our Negro institution, and Florida State University.

There the City of Tallahassee took a rather rigid and punitive position in respect to these demonstrations. And, of course, this gave the appearance of partiality or of nonobjectivity and this caused the conditions to become aggravated and we finally developed conditions there in Tallahassee of which I am frankly ashamed.

Yesterday and the day before there was a tenseness about the atmosphere in Tallahassee that was disgraceful.

We had armed patrolmen, state, county, and city, patrolling every street because we have had the wildest rumors imaginable going on there about what was going to happen.

First a hundred Negro citizens were going to be brought in to augment local forces, then that grew as high as 6,000. First we had large numbers of White Citizens' Council members who were coming in to augment the white forces and that grew up into the thousands. Of course, all that proved to be completely unsound, but our people got worried. They were calling me at night—widows asking me if I thought they would be safe in their homes at night time.

An element of fear is certainly an insidious and a dangerous thing to behold. When I was going back to my office just yesterday noon the highway patrolman who was driving me said, "Governor, I just got word that a bus load of students— Negro students from Alabama—has just pulled into the A. & M. University campus and they've got a lot of baseball bats and they're out to augment the local forces, to put on some sort of a demonstration."

I called the president of the university when I got to the office and he said, "It is true, Governor, we've got a bus load. For a year now we have had a ball game, a baseball game, scheduled with the institution up there in Alabama and the boys are here with their bats to play the ball game." And they played the ball game.

But there were wild rumors about runs on hardware stores for ammunition, about runs for baseball bats, about runs on stores for hammers, knives, screwdrivers, and everything else. A perfectly absurd situation to develop here in our free America, in our free Florida and in our free Tallahassee.

But what is the legal situation about these so-called demonstrations?

First, I want to say this to every one of you: that we are going to have law and order in this state.

I don't care who the citizen is, he is going to be protected in pursuing his legal rights in Florida.

And that goes for every place in Florida.

Now under our free enterprise system and under our laws a

merchant has the legal right to select the patrons he serves. And certainly he is going to be protected in that legal right.

The customer, of course, has the legal right to trade or not to trade with any man he wants to—and, of course, there is the right to demonstrate and the people should be protected in that right, too.

But I want to call to your attention that the right to demonstrate in all cases is limited by the fact that if there is any clear and present danger that that demonstration will incite public disorder, it is unlawful. And, of course, a situation of this kind could bring about that kind of condition in one community and not in another.

Now we have applied that rule. I called on our sheriffs two years ago to apply it against the Ku Klux Klan. While they were planning a perfectly lawful demonstration under normal circumstances, the information we had about the way they were going to conduct that would, I felt, clearly incite disorder and danger and so we called upon the sheriffs to prevent demonstrations of that sort and they did.

But actually, friends, we are foolish if we just think about resolving this thing on a legal basis. In the first place, our merchants have much involved so far as their business prosperity [is concerned]—not to have racial tensions of this order.

Boycotts can be extremely damaging and will be extremely damaging to their businesses. And, of course, any racial tension brings about depression in business and depresses generally the business spirit of any community.

But aside from that we've got some moral rights and we've got some principles of brotherhood that are involved in these issues that I want to talk with you just a little about.

I'm amazed at how different people react differently in this particular area. My own mother and father, I found the other day, don't fully agree on how they feel about race relations. I know my own wife and I have disagreements from time to time about race relations.

And so far as I am personally concerned, I don't mind saying that I think that if a man has a department store and he invites the public generally to come into his department store and trade, I think then it is unfair and morally wrong for him to single out one department, though, and say he does not want or will not allow Negroes to patronize that one department.

Now he has a legal right to do that, but I still don't think that he can square that right with moral, simple justice.

Now you may not agree with that. Strange things develop in respect to these relations. We have a department store there at home, for example, that has a counter where ladies go and buy patterns. Well, white and colored women have been seated, side by side, buying patterns at that counter for 20 years.

Our banks in Tallahassee—and I think everywhere else— have no discriminations whatever in respect to what windows their customers will use. One of our banks has recently initiated a program of serving coffee to all its customers between 10 and 11 o'clock in the morning. And that service is provided without discrimination and there's no special place to sit because that institution feels an obligation to treat all its customers alike.

The whole thing reminds me a little of that old Hindu story about the Blind Men and the Elephant. They didn't know what an elephant was like and so they wanted to find out and one blind man went up and felt the elephant's side and he said, "The elephant is like a wall." Another one went up and he touched the tusk and said, "The elephant's like a spear." The other one went up and felt a leg and said, "The elephant is like a tree." The other one went up and he felt the ear and said, "The elephant is like a fan." The other one went up and he felt the tail and said, "The elephant is like a rope." And so it went.

Each interpreted it as he felt it, but at the same time none of them had any real conception of what an elephant was actually like. Now none of us have all the answers to this situation, friends. I think all of us are part right and part wrong.

We must have more tolerance, more understanding, more Christianity, less words, and less demonstrations, I think, if we are going to find the answer ultimately.

I went to church this morning and I was amazed that the scripture—the gospel—for this third Sunday in Lent which the minister read includes these words from the Master. "But he, knowing their thoughts, said unto them, every kingdom divided against itself is brought to desolation; and a house divided against a house falleth."

How appropriate that scripture was to me on this day because I firmly believe as I hope you will that every state divided against itself, every city divided against itself, every nation divided against itself is bound to come to desolation.

Now that is true for many reasons because when there is division there is suspicion, there is fear, there is distrust, and ultimately there is hate and hate consumes and destroys.

Friends, we must find answers. There is absolutely nothing that can aid the Communists more at this time in establishing supremacy over the United States—and that is their ambition —than racial strife in this country.

I made that statement the other day and somebody said to me, "Yes, I think you are right about that. We understand how that injures our nation for the word to be passed along about our racial strife, but all this could be eliminated if the colored people would just stay in their place."

Now friends, that's not a Christian point of view.

That's not a democratic point of view.

That's not a realistic point of view.

We can never stop Americans from struggling to be free.

We can never stop Americans from hoping and praying that some day in some way this ideal that is imbedded in our Declaration of Independence is one of these truths that are inevitable, that all men are created equal, that that somehow will be a reality and not just an illusory distant goal.

How are we going to work and what are we going to do?

Next week I am going to announce the appointment of a bi-racial committee for this state to succeed the so-called Fabisinski committee which has been working with race relations, but you will recall the unfortunate loss of Judge Fabisinski.

Mr. Cody Fowler of Tampa has agreed to serve as chairman of that new committee. The other members will be announced next week. Mr. Fowler is an outstanding man and will bring to that service great competence. He was the president of the American Bar Association and he has long worked with inter-racial programs in the City of Tampa and was one of the early members of our old Fabisinski committee.

And I want local committees formed in this state. I appeal to those communities—all communities—here and now to establish among your citizens bi-racial committees that can take up and consider grievances of a racial character and that can honestly and sincerely and with a determined effort try to find solutions to these difficulties.

Now the fact that your community has not had any difficulties should not deter you in moving to form this committee because sooner or later you will. We are confronted with a great need in our state to intelligently and reasonably act and to do that I must have the cooperation of the people.

Florida needs you in this program.

We need more reason and less emotion. We need more love and less hate. We need more work and less talk and less demonstrations.

Citizens, please do not fail this great challenge. We are here in the Easter season.

About two years ago the distinguished playwright, Robert Sherwood, wrote a play for Robert Montgomery and it was presented on television. The title of it was "The Trial of Pontius Pilate." The title intrigued me because I had always thought of the events of those fateful times as working around the trial of Jesus and I never had thought in terms of Pontius Pilate being on trial.

But Sherwood in a very logical and in a very reasonable way pointed out that in truth and in fact Pontius Pilate was the man who was on trial. Pontius was a great, big, strong, wonderful man at the court of the Caesars in Rome. He was a comer. Everybody expected him to do great things and to be given great assignments. His wife was one of his greatest boosters. She thought that he would be assigned as the procurator of Egypt, which was the really choice post available at that time. But when the day came for Pontius Pilate to get his assignment, it was to the little insignificant country of Judea and Pontius was furious because he felt that his assignment was not measuring up to his capacity.

But he went on, of course, and undertook it just the same. You remember how the events developed toward the time of the crucifixion; when the Pharisees got Jesus and they were

WE DISSENT : 112

trying their best to pin something on Him that the Romans, of course, would authorize his execution for—and they were having a tough time of it and they were pounding on Pilate's door and trying to convince him that he should get this man and have Him executed—you remember how in those early days Pilate said, "But what's wrong with the man? I don't see, I don't hear anything treasonable about his conduct. Why should we be so disturbed?"

And they said, "Oh, Mr. Pontius Pilate, he's inciting people to riot and disorder. He's creating insurrection. He's a dangerous and he's an evil man." And Pontius said to them, "I was talking to a man who was with him down in the temple yesterday and I asked him about what this man had said and he said that somebody showed him a coin and tried to trap him and said, 'What do you say about Caesar?' And he said in response to that, 'Render unto Caesar the things that are Caesar's and unto God the things that are God's.' Now what's wrong with that?" Pontius asked these advisers.

They said, "Oh, you can't understand this man's attracting a lot of people to follow him. He's creating distrust in your government and in your supervision. You've got to do something about it."

Pontius' wife, Claudia, came into the picture about that time and she said, "Pontius, think carefully about this thing. I was down on the street the other day and I saw this man teaching and I went up because I wanted to hear what he had to say and he said very distinctly that 'I came not to establish a kingdom on earth, but a kingdom in Heaven.' "

And Pontius said, "How could that be treasonable?" But they insisted and about that time they started hearing the cry of the mob outdoors. First it was a soft, "Crucify Him," and then it got stronger, "Crucify Him," and then it got stronger, "Crucify Him," and then something happened to that big, strong man.

He heard the cry of the mob. And he went out on the balcony and there they were just screaming and crying for blood. And that great big man started getting smaller and smaller and smaller. And he grew to be a little, insignificant dwarf. And he said, "Bring me a bowl of water." And when he got the water, he washed his hands in it.

And he said to that crowd, "I will not let the blood of this righteous man be on my hands. I wash my hands of it. See to it yourself."

And they did see to it themselves. They crucified Him.

Friends, we've got mobs beginning to form now, in this nation, in this Southland and in this state. The time requires intelligent, careful, thorough study of big problems, and the reaching of solutions that are going to be reasonable and sound and make good sense.

We cannot wash our hands and let this matter and these issues be decided by the mobs, whether they are made up of white people or whether they are made up of colored people.

And we in this state have this sort of situation: we have got extremists on one side and we've got extremists on the other. We've got this mob shouting here; we've got that mob shouting there.

But where are the people in the middle? Why aren't they talking? Why aren't they working? They must start working. They must start efforts that are going to bring about solutions if we are going to get over these problems and these troubles and keep our state growing as our state should grow.

You remember the little story about the song of the brook?

It said, "Bring me men to match my mountains, bring me men to match my plains, men with empires in their vision and new eras in their brains."

We've got to have men with new eras in their brains. We've got a state to build. We've got a nation to save. And we've got a God to serve. Thank you.

Just so, the governor spoke to his people.

Negro confidence in the governor's good will and fairness was restored, and the sit-in demonstrations ceased throughout Florida. Newspaper editorial writers who had been silent or evasive began appealing for reason and negotiation. So did ministers in their pulpits. People of good will all over the state who had felt intimidated and isolated now began to speak up. The governor received thousands of letters, seven to one in favor of his position. Extremists on both sides were frustrated and immobilized. Islands of moderate leadership began appearing. There was no upheaval, no explosion.

But Governor Collins realized that no vacuum can last long. He put the full prestige and moral force of his office behind the Commission on Race Relations that he had mentioned in his broadcast. Quietly, with the help of legal and sociological staff members, the commission sought to bring Negro and white leaders together, from among law enforcers, businessmen, newspapermen and broadcasters, teachers and clergymen. Conciliation and negotiation took root in city after city, several of which formed their own bi-racial committees patterned after the state commission. At the end of the Collins administration, nine months after the broadcast, the commission's work had enabled a number of communities to begin the orderly desegregation of lunch counters and other public facilities.

The state commission never advocated or opposed desegregation. It counseled calm and intelligent discussion. If action was taken by a community, it was the community's decision. Racial disturbances did develop later, but only where officials refused to discuss grievances through bi-racial committees or similar agencies. For example, the race riots in Jacksonville: they occurred in the only major city in Florida whose mayor took the same rigid stand that had almost provoked disorder and violence in Tallahassee when its officials choose the way of toughness and harshness. H. N.

DAWN IN THE SOUTH

Francis Pickens Miller . . .

Foreign affairs expert, former Virginia legislator, now with the State Department; born in Middlesboro, Ky.; A.B., Washington and Lee University; Rhodes Scholar, Oxford University, B.A., 1921, M.A., 1923; student in the Graduate Institute of International Studies, Geneva, Switzerland, 1927-28; chairman of the World's Student Christian Federation, Geneva, 1928-38; field secretary of the Foreign Policy Association, 1934-35; secretary of the Southern Policy Committee, 1935-40; organization director of the Council on Foreign Relations (N.Y.), 1938-1942; State Department consultant, 1950-52; vice president of the Virginia Committee for Public Schools since 1958; member of the board of the Southern Regional Council since 1959; moderator, Presbyterian Synod of Virginia, 1953-54; member of the Central Committee of the World Council of Churches, 1954-1961; member of Virginia House of Delegates, 1938-41; candidate for governor of Virginia in 1949, and for U.S. Senate in 1952 (running against Senator Byrd's organization); veteran of both world wars, serving as a colonel on the SHAEF staff, 1944-45, and in the military government of Germany, 1945-46; twice awarded Legion of Merit, decorated by Britain, France, and Belgium; author of *The Blessings of Liberty;* co-author of *The Giant of the Western World* and *The Church Against the World.*

Since Virginia has always served as a kind of bellwether for the other states of the Old South, I am going to write about

"Dawn in The South" from the perspective of what has been happening in Virginia.

The dawn that many Southerners have been waiting for is at hand. It has been a long night. Twilight descended in 1832. It was in that year that the great debates took place on slavery in the Virginia Assembly. A resolution to abolish slavery was defeated by a very narrow margin in both the State Senate and the House of Delegates. In the Senate the strength of opposing sides was so evenly balanced that the proslavery forces won one of the key rollcalls by a single vote. If Jefferson had been there he would have remarked that Heaven stood silent in that awful moment.

1832 was the dividing line of southern history. From that day on the forces of liberalism as personified by the spirit of Thomas Jefferson were in full retreat. In the words of Joseph C. Robert, Virginia then took the road from Monticello. We have been traveling that road ever since, and the rest of the South has followed us. When Virginia voted to maintain slavery, the war between the states became inevitable. Appomattox was midnight.

As we took the road from Monticello, what was it that we turned our backs upon? What does Monticello stand for?

Monticello, the name of Jefferson's home, near Charlottesville, Virginia, stands for many things, since Jefferson was an incomparably gifted man with interests as broad and diversified as life itself. In social and political terms, however, Monticello stands primarily for an appeal to reason: for the fullest use of the mind in trying to understand and deal with the forces that are shaping human destiny. The spirit that Monticello represents is the spirit:

That faces forward rather than backward,

That is impelled by curiosity to explore the unknown,

That recognizes the inevitability of change and, while wishing to preserve the best in the past, is more interested in facilitating orderly and creative change than in perpetuating the *status quo,*

That regards every man, regardless of his race or social status, as entitled to equality of opportunity with every other man,

That judges governmental policies and programs primarily by their effect on persons in the light of the inalienable rights and responsibilities of all men, and

That has a decent respect for the opinions of mankind.

This was the spirit which, toward the end of the eighteenth century, had made Virginia synonymous in the minds of many Americans with political wisdom. This was the spirit that created a culture characterized by an unusual amount of decency, courtesy, and fair play. The charm that is still associated with Virginia was derived directly from this culture. So profound was the imprint of that culture on men's minds and habits that traces of it linger on to this day in family life and personal relations. One comes across these traces in the most unexpected places. After a speech I had made on some legislation before the House of Delegates when I was a member of that body in 1938, a page brought me a note from the Speaker that said, "You have spoken more like Mr. Madison today than any other member of this House." Could anything have been more charming than to have served in a state legislature where, as recently as twenty-four years ago, the shades of Madison were still haunting men's thoughts and influencing their personal relations?

As far as public life generally is concerned, however, the intellectual and moral sources of our culture began to dry up more than a century ago. The result has been catastrophic for

Virginia, for the entire South, and for the nation as a whole.

The spirit that developed in Virginia after 1832 was the exact antithesis of Monticello. It was a spirit that preferred to look backward rather than forward, that refused to admit the inevitability of fundamental change and swore to maintain the *status quo*, that thought of some men as being more entitled to opportunity than other men, that judged governmental programs primarily from the standpoint of what were considered sound fiscal policies rather than from the standpoint of their effect on human beings; and it was a spirit that was on the whole completely indifferent to the opinions of mankind.

A friend of mine who thoroughly knows Virginia stopped me on the lawn of the University of Virginia one day several years ago and said, "Pickens, had you heard what happened to Mr. Jefferson when they buried him in July, 1826?" I replied no, that I had not heard. My friend continued, "Well, the undertakers made an awful mistake. They intended to embalm his body, but they embalmed his spirit instead, and it hasn't been seen around here since." "Well," I said, "I guess it's your job and mine to try to disembalm it."

Other spirits have occupied public life in Virginia in recent years but few of them have had the remotest resemblance to the spirit of Thomas Jefferson. In the absence of his spirit the health of the body politic deteriorated and began to suffer from all sorts of illusions and neuroses. As men look backward something happens to their minds comparable to the experience of Lot's wife when she looked back toward Sodom. Thought patterns become stereotyped and frozen when men cease to welcome change and the patterns of the past are repeated even though these may have increasingly little relevance for the needs of the present. It is as if, in reply to an enquiry

about today's world, an electronic secretary mechanically re-
produced a recording made long ago under entirely different
circumstances. In place of fresh or original creative thought
there is all too frequently nothing but parrotlike repetition
of points of view applicable to another age. Recently I read
a speech by an eminent fellow Virginian with which I would
have wholly agreed had I been living and had this speech been
given during the period of the Confederation prior to 1789.
The opinions expressed would have been relevant and appropriate for the world of that time. They were wholly irrelevant
and inappropriate for the world of 1962.

If irrelevant and inappropriate ideas were harmless, this
repetition would not make so much difference. But they are
not. They can do infinite harm, particularly if they are combined in one package with great error, deep sentiment, and
nostalgic reverence for the glories of the past.

The doctrine of interposition is a perfect illustration of the
damage that can be done the body politic by an idea that is
no longer related to actualities but is charged with emotion
from the life and death struggles of long ago. To offer the
people of Virginia and of the South, as a solution for their
problems in the nineteen fifties, a formula of John C. Calhoun
that had been rejected by the nation after one of the bloodiest
civil wars in history, was an act of such colossal irresponsi-
bility as to defy the understanding of a rational mind. Some
of the men who advanced this theory were honest, patriotic
citizens. Others were mere charlatans who gloried in the publicity that their reversion to pre-Civil War thinking secured
for them. But whether the advocates of interposition were
honest or dishonest, they illustrated perfectly the degree to
which the spirit of Jefferson had been embalmed for more than
a century.

During this long dark night of the spirit since 1832, the South and Virginia in particular lost many of its richest possessions. It lost its position of economic power based on cotton and slavery. It lost the intellectual leadership it had displayed in the eighteenth century. But far more tragic than economic or cultural losses was the loss of the flower of its youth. Death on the field of battle deprived the South of the best men that were born between 1820 and 1845. And among those who survived the holocaust, most of the more ambitious and adventurous, those with more energy and initiative, went North or West to seek their fortunes. It has been estimated that during the seventy years between 1865 and 1935 Virginia alone lost around one million of its white citizens through migration to other parts of the country.

Those who remained tended on the whole to be persons with less initiative and energy than those who left, persons who were tolerably well satisfied with things as they were and whose pleasure was derived more from contemplation of the past than from dynamic creation of the future. The result was that until 1930 the life of the Commonwealth was relatively static and quiescent.

In 1930 the population of Virginia was 2,421,851. Now it is over four million. This 66 per cent increase in population during the past thirty years compares with a national increase of 45 per cent during the same period. The differential is some indication of the transformation that is taking place in the character of Virginia society. While a comparable transformation is not general throughout the entire South, it has taken place in many key areas.

What are the forces that have produced this transformation and what are its essential characteristics? These forces are so numerous and so interdependent that it is difficult to isolate them as separate entities. Nor can they be listed as following each other as cause and effect in some kind of chronological sequence. The impressive fact remains that as a result of the action and reaction of the interrelated forces mentioned below, the South has for the past half century been passing through a social revolution unlike that experienced by any other part of the country.

Industrialization has been the prime mover. It began toward the end of the nineteenth century, accelerated after World War I, and since World War II has gone into high gear. With ample raw materials, an abundant supply of potentially skilled workers, and a moderate climate, the South has become a favorite location for many national industries. New factories have not only provided employment for surplus farm populations but in turn have found a rapidly expanding market for their products in the South itself.

Along with industrialization has gone the abolition of one-crop systems (cotton or tobacco) and the diversification of agriculture. The revolution in agriculture, which in turn transformed rural social life, was due in part to the magnificent work of the land grant colleges over the years and in part to New Deal legislation initiated under the leadership of Franklin Roosevelt, to whom the South owes more than to any other President in the past hundred years. But education and legislation alone could not account for what happened. The decisive factor was the new energy and capacity for initiative that manifested itself among rural people. The source of this new energy was not hard to find. For generations pellagra, hook-worm, and malaria had, particularly in the deep South, been endemic and had destroyed the spirit of countless numbers of country boys and girls. That was the price paid for undernourishment, malnutrition, and lack of adequate medical care.

When factories moved in and diversified farming took the place of the one-crop system, diets changed, the standard of living rose, and health returned. With physical well-being came a revitalized spirit. It was easier now to get up and get going. Not only have the people of the South changed in appearance but the appearance of their land has changed even more. To any one who remembers the South of thirty years ago a miracle has occurred during the past generation. The miracle is a miracle of grass, of cattle, of ponds and lakes, of rotating crops, of vegetable gardens, and of painted houses. There was a day in the early part of this century when such sights were rarely seen in the countryside. Now they are commonplace.

As a result of all these changes, new opportunities for employment of every kind opened up on every side. The South could not supply all the manpower needed, particularly in technology and management. Consequently, the outward wave of migration turned and began to flow the other way: from the North and West back into every one of the newly industrialized areas. Literally hundreds of thousands of Americans who were not born in the Old South are now living and working there. Paradoxical as it may seem, there are two counties in Virginia, the state where the first permanent English settlements were made, which have been the fastest growing counties in the nation during the past fifteen years. America's frontier is no longer in the West. It is in the South.

Along with industrial growth and agricultural adjustment has gone a new appreciation of the importance of public schools and universities. The South still lags in its educational institutions as compared to some other areas. But we have made enormous strides in the past thirty years and will make even greater strides in the next thirty.

It often happens in life that the most painful experiences turn out later to be blessings in disguise. The most painful experience for the South since Appomattox and Reconstruction was the aftermath of the Supreme Court desegregation decision of 1954. That decision was right in terms of law and justice and it was inevitable that, sooner or later, some such decision would be handed down. At the same time, in 1954 I wished that the decision could have been postponed for another ten years because I saw a trend in the direction of much better race relations, which I knew would be temporarily reversed by that decision in many communities. This reversal has occurred. The hatred expressed in Little Rock, New Orleans, and Birmingham has chilled our hearts and haunted our minds.

However, the current mood in many communities is not the last word. By the grace of God and the efforts of men of good will, hatred will in time pass and a new trend in the direction of improved race relations will set in again. Meanwhile, one great good has come out of the tragic period through which we have been passing, and it is this: Thoughtful and intelligent Southerners have been forced by these dire events to face the reality of the world in which they live and to begin to come to terms with that reality.

Virginia began to come to terms with that reality in the winter of 1959 when, at a special session of her General Assembly, she turned away from the policy of "massive resistance" previously adopted and turned towards a policy of "freedom of choice." By an irony of history, in rejecting "massive resistance," the vote in the Assembly was as close (a margin of one in the Senate) as it was when the Assembly rejected the motion to abolish slavery 127 years before. This vote like the other was a turning point in Southern history. By this vote, after misleading the segregationists of the Deep South for several years, Virginia walked out on them and associated herself with the more moderate position that North Carolina had taken from the first. The tide had turned. The dawn began to break. Since that vote the spirit of Monticello has begun to reassert itself in many metropolitan areas. Atlanta has set a magnificent example; so have Dallas and Memphis, while New Orleans has learned the lesson of Little Rock.

The civilized world knows that where two races inhabit the same territory, the law of God and the law of Man both require that as far as public services are concerned, every individual must be treated like every other individual regardless of race. This is the reality of the situation to which the South is now beginning to adjust. The process of readjustment is naturally difficult for a large number of people. But many a school and university has discovered, after being desegregated, that the process was not nearly so difficult or painful as the demagogues and the ignorant had foretold it would be. And the same thing can be said of riding buses.

Given the present world situation, the most effective propaganda that the United States can use in Asia, Africa, and Latin America is the story of desegregation in such cities as Atlanta, Dallas, and Memphis. The die-hard segregationists and massive resisters, on the other hand, continue to provide the Communists with their most effective propaganda against us. Sensing these facts, patriotic citizens throughout the South are increasingly aware of what their loyalty to the United States means and what it requires of them in the area of race relations.

The 1954 Court decision not only made many a Southerner

confront the reality of the modern world for the first time; it also created a situation that compelled him to re-examine his conscience.

Further, for the hundreds of thousands who had been at some time or other inducted into the Armed Forces it was a potent reminder of the oath they had taken on that occasion to defend the Constitution of the United States against all enemies, foreign and domestic. The significance of the word "domestic" in the area of race relations acquired new meaning for countless men and women as they meditated on their oath, and as they meditated further on the glorious heritage of the bill of rights enshrined in their Constitution, which they share with all other Americans. As a result of having faced these facts and examined their consciences, there are probably today a larger proportion of Southerners who are genuinely and unreservedly proud of being citizens of the United States of America than there have been at any time for the past century and a quarter. We can thank the Russians in part for this. But we can also thank our churches and our courts. This is in itself a very great thing. A new day is at hand and I am full of hope.

I am full of hope mainly because of the younger generation I see coming on in the South. This new generation knows the world far better than their fathers did. Many of the ablest have traveled and studied abroad and countless additional thousands have served overseas in military or civilian capacities.

There are also some among the younger generation in the South (I do not know how many, but I do know there are some) who seem to me to understand better than their fathers the meaning and relevance for our time of the Christian doctrine of man. The young men and women I have in mind have sensitive consciences as a result of the agony through which the human race is going, and they are also dedicated to the same dream of America that came to Thomas Jefferson and Abraham Lincoln.

Finally, in Virginia I find among these young people many who are determined to build a two-party system. That should not be difficult in the years ahead. The "organization men" who are now being spawned throughout the South are by instinct Republican and their political influence has already become decisive in many metropolitan areas, such as Richmond, Roanoke, and Charlotte. Further, as far as Virginia is concerned, the Democratic Party has been much weakened in recent years by the fact that its most powerful leaders, while calling themselves Democrats to get elected, have usually voted with the Republicans in Washington. Over a period of time prior to 1952, the senior Senator from Virginia, for example, had, on key issues, voted more regularly with the majority of Republicans in the Senate than Senator Robert A. Taft himself.

The practice of telling the folks at home that you belong to one team and then, after accepting and enjoying the offices and honors pertaining to such membership, using your position on that team in Washington to throw the game to the opposing team, has naturally confused the electorate, rendered party affiliations increasingly meaningless, and deprived political activity of all integrity. The result is that Democratic loyalties have eroded to such an extent that, as far as national elections are concerned, Virginia is now definitely in the Republican column. Further, it is only a question of time until many citizens who have formed the habit of voting Republican nationally will begin to vote Republican locally. This is already happening in various Virginia communities. Consequently, it seems probable that Virginia Democrats who continue to be loyal to the national Party will find themselves in

WE DISSENT : 128

a minority for some years to come. A similar development may be expected in some of the other Southern States.

I am confident, however, that in due course the tide will turn and young leaders will appear in Virginia and throughout the South resolved to build a party freer from the dead hand of the past and more in step with the national Democratic Party. When these young men and women take over the leadership in their respective states, the spirit of Jefferson will live again.

INTO THE MODERN WORLD

James McBride Dabbs . . .

President of the Southern Regional Council; member of the Fellowship of Southern Churchmen; elder in the Presbyterian Church; former teacher of college English; author of *The Southern Heritage* (winner of the Brotherhood Award of the National Conference of Christians and Jews) and *The Road Home;* operator of Rip Raps Plantation, near Mayesville, S.C.

Some say that I dissent from the South. But as strange as it sounds, I am hardly conscious of dissenting from the South at all. It dissents from me. I'm reminded of the old marching song, "They're all out of step but Jim."

Apparently I march to a drummer they don't hear. Or hear but fitfully and dimly. If I thought they didn't hear him at all, I wouldn't be trying to indicate his drumming. I think they do hear him, however, because he's a Southern drummer, though with universal reverberations.

At least, he seems so to me. The music I march to is as Southern as the scene beyond my window this late August morning, a scene observed first more than sixty years ago: the shadows among the pines, the sunlight touched with a haze that betokens autumn, the deep woods beyond, and the steady high singing of cicadas in the trees. So Southern that it rises from the earth itself and from my heart.

On my father's side I belong to the fifth generation of South Carolinians, on my mother's, the sixth. My father's people were, from the 1750's I think, small farmers; my mother's, from about 1800, plantation owners. Historically this was the South: farm and plantation balanced each other. It was this uncertain and changing balance that helped to give the South its character.

With the marriage of my parents, these two forces joined. This might not have been significant if they hadn't been typical of their economic and cultural backgrounds. My father was the yeoman farmer, on the make, aggressive, hot-tempered, democratic, impatient of the complacent plantation people around him. In true Jacksonian spirit he used to say, "Every man is as good as every other man, and maybe a dern sight better." My mother was quiet, assured, with a warm paternalism appropriate to the plantation, too richly endowed to be complacent but from a complacent background, too vital to dream of the past but with the past clinging like an aura about her. It was her brother who once remarked to an aunt, "Ideals are a sin, Alice; we should love God."

Now, it also happened that I inherited almost equally from each of my parents: the acquiescence of my mother, the aggressiveness of my father. These two opposing attitudes have so fused in me that there is no conflict, though there is perhaps a tension. I am interested in the old and the new, in continuity and change. I do not expect the form of the future to copy the form of the past; this would leave no room for creation. I search the past for creative hints. My mother, and my mother's plantation, gave me the sense of order, attainment, rest; and, though my father's driving ambition never let me think that the plantation might be carried into the future unchanged, it never blinded me to the kind of thing I sought: order, attainment, rest. I move into the future, therefore, unhampered by the forms of the past, but guided by the spirit the past has revealed to me. Whenever my father's urgency carries me forward too fast, I hear my mother's quiet words, "Now, Jamie" —she was a McBride; and whenever the complacency of her people slows me down, I hear my father's voice, "All right, Son, let's get on with the job."

But there's even more than this. Though my father and mother were of opposing temperaments and backgrounds, and the air was sometimes tense between them, I never doubted that they loved each other devotedly. It was this enveloping love that fused within me the two so opposing parts of my nature, creating thus a harmony from what might have been a fatal struggle. I have therefore moved through the world seeking primarily the form of love. I sought it first in individuals, I seek it now, more largely, in the South, and perhaps even in the world. The main problem in the South is, What is the form of love here? What is to be loved here? That there is something, indeed much, I have no doubt. For I look backward through my father and my mother and see through and in them the South, in spite of all its absurdities the balanced South; and it is nonsense to think there is little to be loved here.

This is one of our great weaknesses. We do not love the South enough. I know we're passionate about it, we feel we're devoted to it, we'll fight for it at the drop of a hat—and drop the hat ourselves. But it's a defensive love, a love expressed too often as distrust and fear of outsiders, a love that does not know its object, a misdirected, ignorant love. What is love's true form in the South? If we had more to cherish, we should have less to attack.

As for my defending the South, I'm too busy in the spirit of my father trying to bring it nearer to what in the spirit of my mother I feel it is. I'm not trying to reform it; I have little interest in such a moral problem. I'm trying to form it, to help it find its form. For it can be argued that the South has never come into its own, never reached maturity, never become the great region the devotion of its people should have made it. Its problem is the aesthetic one, to imagine and become what essentially it is. This problem the South should be able to face, for she was always rather long on manners—an aesthetic interest—and short on morals.

As for the South's failure to attain maturity, this is related to the fact that the region began to become conscious of itself in about 1820, at the time of the Missouri Compromise: this political event made it clear to the South that it differed from the rest of the country. But the awareness came chiefly from a sense of outside hostility, a hostility shortly to become tense and vociferous under the leadership of William Lloyd Garrison. The South had no quiet time in which to become self-conscious. It really became so only at the moment of its destruction and as the Lost Cause.

It is impossible, therefore, for contemporary Southerners to look backward and say that at such and such a time we were what we would like to be. Of course, this is a foolish wish anyhow; no individual or people can go back to an earlier day. But our contemporary Southerner cannot gain from the past even the image of what he once was. For he never really was, he was always, under great pressure, becoming, until in his adolescence he was destroyed.

We are still in our adolescence. Of course, from the European point of view, all Americans are. Here the South has the great advantage over other American regions: she has a history of such tragic depth and varied nature that she stands now upon the very brink of maturity. She could grow up over-night. She could come to herself, and then her deep and swirl-ing emotions would take form; then she would know who she is and where she is going; she would distrust and hate the world less and love herself more. She would find a form con-ducive to love, her true form, wherein, perhaps, would be combined, as we shall see, the urgency of my father and the peace of my mother. I should like to help her do this.

My mother's people looked backward, my father's forward. Within twenty feet of where I now sit, on the piazza here at Rip Raps, I heard my mother's mother say shortly before she died in 1915 that she had never been Reconstructed and didn't intend to be. One of her sisters, a maiden lady, was an early teacher of mine. There was no U.S. flag above the school-house, but the inner walls of the tiny building were plastered with the various Confederate flags, and every Friday after lunch we sang Confederate songs. For the most part, however, the Lost Cause aroused in me only a faint nostalgia, which I still feel. Back at home, however, was my father, his mother, and her brother, a gray-bearded Confederate veteran, and their eyes were on the present and the future. My father's mother was still sitting on the piazza at ninety-four, watching the buggies pass along the public road at the far edge of the field, waiting for ten o'clock and the morning paper. My grand-uncle, the old Confederate, attending the Charleston Exposition in 1902, was so enthralled by all the possible inven-tions sketched there that he wanted to live twenty-five, fifty, even a hundred years longer—indeed, he said, he'd like to live to see the whole thing wound up!

What was I to do, balanced thus between the past and the future? I did what the South, more or less, has always done: I lived in the present. Of course, every child does, but I never got over it. Because of this, Emerson's aphorism when I came upon it hit home: "Life only avails, not the having lived." Because of this, at twenty-eight I was examining the poetic experience under John Erskine, and at thirty-eight lecturing to a college group on the poetry of life.

Though I did not know it then, this was a basic Southern interest. The South has had few poets. Why? Partly because she was always trying to be poetic. Life itself, living, the present moment always appealed. W. J. Cash calls this our hedonism. Time, which moved slowly anyhow through the hot summers and the mild winters, moved more slowly because men enjoyed looking at what they saw and passing the time together. If the South still possesses, even for strangers, some indefinable magic, it is because Southerners have cared for it, observed it, and, however inadequately and foolishly, loved it. In brief, have created it. It is their poem. When, therefore, I began to study the poetry of life, trying to understand how certain moments take form and imprint themselves upon our mind, I was only holding up for examination the moments the South had always cherished.

Meanwhile, I had been led beyond the poetry of life into its tragedy. Led again by John Erskine, who introduced me to Unamuno's *The Tragic Sense of Life*; led by Unamuno, who told me what was happening to me; but led, I am sure, not simply as an individual but also as a Southerner: a romantic desiring the impossible, a stoic awaiting the inevitable. I remember my father's saying to me approvingly in the spring of 1918, when I was first in love, "Son, you make me feel young again, you're as big a fool as I was." But I also remember him sitting on the front piazza in a May of my boyhood watching the storm beating down the yellow oats and never saying a word. Still silent, he got up and walked indoors. But even before this, when I was a little boy, I had stumbled upon a strange sense of the sadness of life. My parents spoke occasionally of someone's having lost a child. I didn't know what they meant, but since, if children were to be lost, the dark, endless woods back of the house would be the place for losing, I imagined them there, not frightened but each of them alone, the woods starred with lost, wandering children. Was this image some faint premonition against the time when I myself should be lost in the dark woods of the world? Was I inoculating myself against sadness long before its coming? More important than this, was I entering life with the pathos of an old defeat, enshrined in my grandmother and in the still unfurled Confederate banners, hanging like a mist about my boyish head?

However I came to realize the tragedy of life, whether simply as an individual or also as a Southerner conditioned by Southern history, I came to realize it, and finally to pass in some measure beyond it. When my loss, accentuated perhaps by my boundless romantic desire, became great enough, I put off the heavy armor of stoicism I had seen my father wearing, admitted at least to myself my own defenselessness, and chose to walk naked in the world. With this came a kind of compassion, both for myself and for every man, poor devils all. Perhaps I became a Christian. At least, as good a Christian as I had been a stoic.

Several years before this, I had been called by the minister of our Presbyterian church "a good pagan." This was after he had read an essay of mine, "The Religion of a Countryman." I think he was right. For the religion I described there as my own was the religion of a *paganus*, a countryman, who was deeply aware of the more than human forces that hung, silent or clamorous, in the sunlight or the storm, but practically unaware of the compassion that according to Jesus lies beyond all human expression even in the heart of God.

But now, in my new sense of compassion for myself and for all men, I came to feel that compassion was a universal quality. Now, for the first time, human hopes hung like bright veils in the air, qualifying the sunlight. Now, for the first time, I understood a faint, premonitory experience I had had as a boy of twelve. It was a coldish morning in September, the first day of school. My brother, my mother, and I stood on the back piazza, looking across the yard through the pines to the barn and the rosy dawn. We had drunk a cup of coffee together, Mother having brewed it for us, and she was now sending us out to do the milking. As a little boy I had called her "Mother Lady." In that September moment there was something, oh, so faint, of the Lady in the Dawn, something of the Dawn in the Lady. Now, twenty-six years later, I was sure of it. One spirit pervaded them both; the god of the fields and the god of the fireside were one.

Therefore, when some years later I came back to live in my boyhood community, it was now not simply the site of the home wherein I had learned from my father urgency, from my mother peace. It was also mortised in the granite of the globe, with a window looking out upon the universe; it was the place where I had first seen, and therefore most deeply felt though for a long time not understood, the Lady in the Dawn and the Dawn in the Lady.

How could I dissent from all this? That would be insanity. I should be dissenting from myself, my parents, the South as I understood it, even the universe itself.

But I do dissent from the South—at least from much of the contemporary white South—on the race issue. Perhaps it is clear now, since I have listed the things I assent to, why I am not disturbed by my dissent from so many white Southerners on this issue. The trouble is, of course, that dissent on this issue is for them dissent from the South itself. I think they are mistaken. Though the race issue is related to practically everything in the South, it is not the South. Nor is segregation, that tentative solution of the issue, our way of life as it has been called. I think I have said enough, implicitly or explicitly, about the South to indicate why I cannot believe this.

Though I am opposed to segregation, I did not myself raise the issue. I'm not enough of an idealist. For forty years I went along with the custom of the country, only occasionally aware of its existence and then with little concern. But when time— to be exact, the 1940's—raised the issue, I faced it, and decided against segregation. Why?

I had decided against it without knowing it a half dozen years before in that tragic moment when, having lost as I thought all, I became aware that in this tragic situation I was a human being, and found myself moved with compassion both for myself and for all other men. In that moment only people mattered; there was no hint of race. When, therefore, race became an issue for my fellow-Southerners, it was not an issue for me. I had learned that I was a man, a destiny heavy enough without burdening it with the issue of race. So far as I was concerned, to be rid of segregation, which emphasized race, would be good riddance.

Why does it not seem good riddance to so many Southerners? Partly because they do not see the South as I see it. To them segregation is the core of the South, to me it's an excrescence. Which is it?

Regardless of the number of white Southerners who believe —or think they believe—that segregation is the core of the South, time, and not too much of that, will prove it an excrescence. For this is the predominant will of the Negroes, of the nation, in a sense of the world. It's the Civil War situation all over again, Even after every Confederate had killed his accepted quota of ten Yankees, the Yankees still came. So, today, the forces against the stand-pat South are too strong. So far as the passing of segregation is concerned, it doesn't make much difference whether I assent or dissent.

But so far as the success of the South is concerned, it does make a difference. We are going into a future vastly different from our past even if we have to be forced into it. But this is little comfort to one who loves the South. I should like for us to go with heads up, even with banners flying, though not the dear Confederate banners of my boyish days. But in order to do this we must understand ourselves, what we are and can become, what part, therefore, we can play in the modern world. We must shape ourselves in the form we desire. I said earlier that the South, with all its passionate regional devotion, had never understood itself. Here are energies not only going to waste but also being used to shackle us to a frozen past. We think we believe that segregation is the core of our life. I do not think we really believe it; we are using words. If we could see the South for what it is, a region where men have striven greatly, endured greatly, and yet have managed through it all to keep a sense of human values, a sense of personal relationships so lacking in the modern world, a sense even of manners in a world gone mad for material gain, a sense of humor, sometimes playful, sometimes wry—if we could see our tragic history, whites and Negroes involved together in more than two centuries of defeat, partly self-inflicted, partly inflicted by the world, then we should come to realize that we have resources here valuable to both the nation and the world, and that segregation is not one of them. I dissent from this narrow, limited view of the South. I assent, with all my heart, to the South that my life here has revealed to me: the incomparably rich South I have just suggested.

We have been haunted by a past lost beyond recalling but lingering still on the far hills of memory. When we turn to the present, especially if it be summer, romantic sentimentalists still, we fill the landscape with beauty queens, a dime a dozen, without ever realizing what we're doing. A woman's beauty *is* a storm-tossed banner—it was Yeats who said it—and under it wisdom stands. There is wisdom in the broad slumbrous landscape of the South, wisdom in the feeling we have for manners—the way you do things, the way you hold your mouth—wisdom in the appearance and the carriage of men and women. There was a touch of splendor in the Old South, though we paid too much for it; perhaps some of it remains. We are moving now into a world where we could have it without penalizing anybody. Have we forgotten the quality?

These are random suggestions, poured out pell-mell. The point of it all is my belief that most of us, even though intending the best, are false to ourselves, false to our history, false to the great possibilities that lie around us. Defending segregation as our way of life, we sell the South short. Have we lived here three hundred years to accomplish only this? I don't believe it.

Can the South be persuaded to accept such an interpretation? I don't know. Would I have come to it myself if life hadn't pulled me up and made me consider? However much I was prepared, both individually and by my upbringing as a Southerner, to receive this interpretation, I came to it out of my own tragic experience. Through that experience I learned the power that lies in failure understood and accepted; by that experience I was prepared to recognize the enormous resources that have accumulated in the South through centuries of frustration and defeat. Can we understand the potential power that lies at hand for a defeated people unless we ourselves have been defeated? Again, I don't know.

But, then, we have all been defeated in greater or less degree. And we still face the sunrise. This is one of Faulkner's themes: endurance. This the South has. The white South and the colored South. The South. There's a classic story about one of Jackson's famous foot-cavalrymen in which endurance and wry humor are incomparably mixed. The General, riding back along the column, came upon a soldier, too old to fight, nearly gone but still slogging. "Well Soldier," said the General, "I hope you'll make out." "Yes, General, yes, I'll make it. But, General—I hopes to God I never loves another country!" Committed to a cause, ruined in its service, he could still smile at his own devotion.

I am not ready to believe that the region that produced a soldier like that—and he was one of many—cannot produce the men to lead us proudly into the modern world.

THE SIGN
ON THE HIGHWAY

Borden Deal . . .

Novelist; born and reared in North Mississippi; after attending Macedonia Consolidated High School near Myrtle, Miss., beat about the country, living in hobo jungles, working on a showboat and for a circus, joining the Civilian Conservation Corps; worked for the Department of Labor in Washington, D.C., where he started his first novel, which was not published; in the Navy during World War II; graduate of the University of Alabama, where he studied creative writing under Hudson Strode; author of more than a hundred short stories published in magazines and books here and abroad, including *The Saturday Evening Post, Best American Short Stories, Collier's, Virginia Quarterly Review, Story Magazine,* and many others, and of five novels, *Walk Through the Valley,* (honorable mention, American Library Assn. Liberty & Justice Awards), *Dunbar's Cove* (which won him a Guggenheim Memorial Fellowship), *The Insolent Breed* (headed for Broadway under the aegis of Kermit Bloomgarden); *Dragon's Wine;* and *The Spangled Road,* a circus novel, which was published in the Spring of 1962 (his novels have been translated into more than a dozen languages); lives in Tuscaloosa, Alabama.

On the main highway leading into my town, as in all towns throughout the United States, civic organizations such as Rotary International and the Lions Club and the Chamber of Commerce have erected signs proclaiming their existence and welcoming the stranger to the city. Among these signs on the outskirts of my town, unlike most other American towns, there is a sign erected by the local Klavern of the Ku Klux Klan.

The Ku Klux Klan has always been a thing of the night, present but unacknowledged, hiding behind anonymity and fear. But there it is; standing blandly among the others, so commonplace that the traveling stranger takes a quick second look to be sure he really saw it.

Yet there is a difference, not immediately apparent, between this sign and the other signs. It is made of heavy-gauge steel; the post is massive and strong, and it is embedded in a block of concrete in the earth. Where the other signs are flimsy and vulnerable, this sign is as strong and permanent as a tank trap.

When the sign was first erected a couple of years ago, it was immediately torn down by indignant citizens. The Ku Klux Klan posted guards but the sign still continued to disappear. And even after it was fabricated of heavy-gauge steel and embedded in concrete, so that it would require a bulldozer to move it, time and again paint was splashed over the face of the sign so that, in addition to the guards, it was necessary to swathe the sign in a plastic bag to protect it from defacement.

The fact of the Ku Klux Klan signs on the outskirts of Southern towns has been widely publicized; but the fact of the local indignation, the resistance to their presence, is not known. These two facts are symbolic of the whole problem of the South. The invisible empire has become visible under the stresses of these latter years. But, unknown to the world, a silent resistance to the extremes of racial passion and prejudice has grown in the South. It is a minority of opinion. But its strength is growing day by day. It is, to my mind, the one great hope of civil peace in the South.

It is silent: because it is in the middle, buffeted by the two extremes of the racial problem: because it is uncertain of its own strength, sometimes of its own convictions: because it is composed principally of those who are more thinkers than actors, by their very nature. And it is silent, primarily, because communication has ceased in the South, and each man in this problem is truly an island of thought unto himself.

A great deal has been written about the lack of communication between the white and the Negro races. But the more important failure is the failure of communication between white and white. It has become almost impossible to discuss the problem of segregation-integration because the problem has moved out of the realm of rationalism into that of emotion.

This is true North as well as South. During the time of the Little Rock troubles I was in New York. One day I had a luncheon-interview with a well-known literary columnist. The columnist, without ever bothering to inquire concerning my own sympathies and beliefs, devoted the entire time to a belligerent diatribe against me and against the South. He was quite as guilty of categorizing and stereotyping as the most virulent racist.

Tennessee Williams, probably our finest playwright, wrote a bad play, *Sweet Bird of Youth*, that was a success because it pandered to the racial appetites of its Broadway audience. In this play, Tennessee Williams yielded himself to demagoguery and race-baiting—on the other side of the question—as much as though he were a Southern politician running for office.

It is easy to live in the North and reflect the popular facile insistence on immediate installation of full civil rights for the Negro in the South. It is easy to live in the South and join the majority in its resistance to such civil rights as voter registration and school integration. But it is very difficult indeed to retain one's sense and one's sensibility in the roaring tides of extremism and passion on both sides. I search desperately within my own thoughts for a startling and original conclusion, a definitive statement of the racial question, and I find only a cloudy and confused state of mind. And, often, I wonder why I, out of my milieu and, it seems, alone among my contemporaries, have arrived at such an uncomfortable emotional and intellectual conclusion.

I am a Southerner. I love the South, exasperating though it can be sometimes. I would wish to live nowhere else. I like the eccentricity and the singularity of the South, the individual structure of its life and its language. We are the last to succumb to the homogenization of American life. We are sometimes parlous in culture, for we seem to write more books than we read; but Southern life is at the same time rich and satisfying. We can be provincial; but not as provincial and insular as New York. We can often display a generosity of the heart and the spirit, a breadth of the mind, unusual in any culture and any time.

Yet I often find myself at odds with my region. The growing conservatism of the South is a saddening thing; its susceptibility to demagoguery, its stiff-necked stubbornness in the winds of change, its smugness and hypocrisy.

Though I have lived and traveled over the United States, though I lived abroad for a number of years, I have returned permanently, I hope, to the South. For the South, in both its good and its bad, is the cradle of my talent and because it would be a surrender to move away, as so many of my persuasion have done.

I was reared in the hills of North Mississippi, about thirty miles northeast of William Faulkner. My father, a good man, voted for Bilbo every time he ran for office. He would have voted for Bilbo for President if he had been given the opportunity. All our friends and neighbors felt the same. Bilbo would come to New Albany once during each campaign. He would stand on the courthouse steps, snap his galluses, and holler "Nigger" so loud you could hear him to the Alabama line. He would tell a little story about how he gave some Yankee Nigger his comeuppance in Washington, D.C., and the throng would laugh and feel as pleased as if they'd done it themselves. And North Mississippi would be secure for Bilbo once again.

There were few Negroes in our section, but they were kept firmly in what was considered their place. A neighbor of ours was regarded with considerable awe because, some ten years before my birth, in our one local lynching, he had been the first man to throw a match. There was also a tale that the mob had broken the Negro's hip in the process of lynching him and that, in the years that followed, each and every man who had taken an active part in the lynching had suffered a broken hip. Our neighbor had such a broken hip.

This atmosphere of accepted racial repression was the milieu of my growing up. Yet, somehow, my father was never able to teach me the difference between a Negro man and a white man. I persisted, in spite of explanations and whippings, in addressing elderly Negroes with a respectful "Sir" and "Ma'am" instead of the accepted "Uncle" and "Aunt." My father had taught me to show respect for age, but I was stupid

about distinguishing between white age and black age. I remember that once I infuriated my father, during the progress
of such an incident, by defending myself in saying, "But he's
a man, isn't he?"

One of my most cherished playmates during those years
was a Negro boy who belonged to a local mule trader. The
mule trader had won him from his father in a crap game, had
brought him home to raise him as a mule boy. Little Book was
not permitted to play with the white boys, and no Negro
children lived near his master's place. Often I would slip off to
play with Little Book, for he was one of the most inventive
Cowboys-and-Indians elaboraters I knew. He was also one of
the few people I knew who loved to read and he was a prolific
source of magazine swaps. The friendship came to an end
when Little Book became self-conscious and unilaterally ter-
minated the relationship.

The atmosphere of racial antagonism and discrimination
was accepted, basically, by both black and white; at that time
and that place there was not even a question of change. Yet,
for some inexplicable reason, though I was a child of my
time and my place, it did not rub off on me. I have never in
my life had to go through the painful process of emotionally
and intellectually shucking off these old prejudices and habits
of mind because, somehow, I had never acquired them in the
first place.

I think the key to my escape was the sense of human dignity given to me by my mother and father. They were both
gentle people, with a strong sense of human individuality.
They were courteous people in the old-fashioned sense, and
I can never remember either of them placing any other person in a position that would be uncomfortable or embarrassing.
They felt, and they taught their children to feel, that every

man must have a small space about him into which no other human being has the right to intrude.

Though they had the prevailing racial prejudice, in their contacts with Negroes they themselves respected this basic human dignity. Though he would never have allowed a Negro to enter his house through the front door, I never heard my father speak any more harshly or unkindly to a Negro than to any other human being.

It was this lesson that I learned from my parents, not the other lesson about racial prejudice. Perhaps even in my childhood I recognized the essential contradiction and in my simplicity I could not contain both. I was only fortunate in absorbing the best of the dichotomy.

Yet I am, as is every individual in the South, embroiled willy-nilly in the current struggle. The basic question has been decided, the emotional attitudes have been taken; the problem is no longer amenable to reason. You will rarely hear in the South, any more, the basic arguments for and against segregation.

The white majority has, of course, decided emotionally for segregation, in defiance of the national consensus. The Negro majority has decided emotionally for integration. The white minority has accepted, with varying degrees of enthusiasm, the basic necessity and inevitability of eventual integration. It is in this latter group that the question will eventually be decided, and it is in this group that complexity and confusion prevail; not over the basic question, but over the practical means of obtaining social justice. They are disturbed and swayed by the excesses of both extremes of opinion and action.

I am in no position to comment on the Southern Negro attitude. I am distrusted by the Southern Negro quite as much as if I belonged to the local Klavern. There is no communication between me and the Southern Negro. One of the great friends I have, a person for whom I have a deep fondness and who, I believe, has a fondness for me, is a Negro grocery clerk in a small town where I lived some years ago. Yet we have never talked with each other about the racial question. This, I think, is a bad thing.

I am in no position to comment on the attitude of the die-hard segregationist. I am deeply distrusted and, perhaps, even hated by these, because I refuse to take my stand on the side of violence to defend the customs of the South. These, too, live in a different world. And this, I think, is a bad thing.

And, indeed, I can speak with no confidence for the white minority, for I know that in the white minority there is a range of opinion and belief and feeling that may or may not coincide with my own. Even among the silent minority, communication is rare, for we tend to be cautious and exploratory with each other. We have all been too often shocked by discovering resistance, or even fanaticism, where we had expected some degree of emotional realism. And this, to my mind, is the worst thing of all.

So, in the end, we come only to speaking for ourselves. We are buffeted between the extremes, distrusted by black and white alike, repelled by excesses on both sides, yet, basically, we are men of good will. We are not activists, we are lovers of civil peace, and, perhaps, some of us merely wish for the matter to be settled so that we need no longer fear for violence in our streets.

We can only make a daily effort to retain our emotional and intellectual footing among the contradictions of our own thoughts and feelings, and against pressures from every side. We must become accustomed to feeling the earth shift under our feet, and to feeling our feet shifting on the earth of our belief. We can only flinch at the assault on human dignity whenever and wherever it occurs. And this is highly necessary, for it is among the men of good will that the fate of the South will be decided.

It is the contradictions that involve us most of all. A single hard attitude is impossible because of those very contradictions and inconsistencies and injustices on every side. As I have said before, I cannot speak for the white majority, the black majority, or even for the white minority. I can speak only of contradictions out of my own human contradictions, as an individual voice.

I believe that, first of all, the Negro expects too much of the South. I can understand the expectation, as a manifestation of revolutionary fervor, for the Negro has put into the drive for racial equality the fervor he once exhibited only in his religion. In the days of wartime, we yearn for a perfect peace. But the expectation of a perfect peace can only be disappointing and I believe that the Negro will never realize a perfect victory in the South—or anywhere in the world.

I cannot expect the Negro to be as dispassionately objective in this conclusion as I, for it is not my civil rights that are involved, except insofar as my rights are damaged by the denial of any man's rights. But I believe that the Negro can expect from the South only that segregation be removed from the structure of the laws, not that it be removed from the human heart. This latter is a consummation devoutly to be wished. But nowhere, North or South, has it been realized, nor is it likely to be realized in the foreseeable future. The expectation of the ideal is unrealistic and, eventually, self-defeating. The greatest danger to the Negro in his drive for justice is the loss of tacit agreement from the white minority. If ever he goes to the extreme of losing this support, then he has lost the war.

Secondly, I believe that a basic mistake has been made in concentrating the battle primarily in education and in transportation. I think the vote and economic equality are much more important.

Especially the vote. In the present situation, the politician who hollers "Nigger" the loudest automatically wins. I think even Bilbo would have been ashamed of some of the political tactics that are now being used in the South. I become utterly ashamed of the human race when I see politician after politician cynically manipulating the racial question; and in his cynical opportunism defeating better men so utterly that the better men are forever barred from politics. Practically every political race in the South is being decided on this basis, and this basis alone. It is sickening to the human heart to realize that the Southern mind and the Southern vote can be swayed with such palpable and cynical manipulation. These demagogues are intelligent men. They know exactly what they are doing. The Southern politicians are responsible, by their tacit offer of police immunity, for most of the recent violence in the South.

Unfortunately, this is beginning to operate on the national level also. During the last Presidential campaign the Republican party made a deliberate play for the Southern vote by quietly promising less emphasis on civil rights, more understanding of the Southern position. And, after the election came out so close, the Republican high command tried to make a deal for enough Southern elector support to take the Presidency.

At the present time, the increasing appeal in the South of Barry Goldwater and the Radical Right groups such as the

John Birch Society is based firmly on their catering to the Southern opposition to civil rights. It is still too early to tell whether this gambit will succeed.

It will be a definite victory for the human mind when the Southern politician can no longer run on the simple-minded platform of hollering "Nigger" louder than the other man. And this victory can be gained only through the winning and the exercise of the vote.

One of the most noticeable changes in the South in recent years has been the visibly increasing self-pride of the Negro race. There was a time when, through poverty and through the necessity of maintaining a protective Negro image, the Southern Negro dressed poorly, evidencing little pride in appearance. This is no longer true, partly because of increasing self-consciousness of their worth and dignity, but also because of their increased economic opportunities. It is rather ridiculous in this democracy to speak of anyone "earning" civil rights; but the practical fact is that the Southern Negro *must* earn each small advance in his status. By increasing his economic stature, he increases also his human stature and for this reason the economic face of the struggle is of great importance.

As I am disturbed by night-rider and bus-station violence, and by the deliberate failure of police protection, on the one side, I am disturbed also by the evidences of extremism on the other. Latterly, the danger of the mature, thoughtful Negro leader losing the reins of leadership to rash and impatient younger men has suddenly threatened the entire accomplishment of the past decade. The Black Muslims can come nearer to destroying the Negro race than ever the Ku Klux Klan.

Passive resistance has been the most valuable weapon of the Negro in the South. It is almost incredible that such a discipline could be maintained among any group of individuals; but the Negro leaders have, until lately, been able to do so. The Negro must, perforce, push for civil rights. But he must push with sublety and intelligence, he must deny to himself the anger and the violence permitted to the other side. This is a terrible burden; but it is as necessary as the cross.

I know that gradualism has become, to the Negro, a dirty word. The fact is that any human achievement in any age has been a gradual thing and it is unrealistic to expect anything else. The rational answer is that the Southern white majority are morally and legally wrong in their stand for the *status quo*. But we must remember that neither the problem nor the solution lies within rationalism. We are dealing here with the shadow side of human nature, where irrationalism is a fact as evident as a test tube in a laboratory.

We must, North and South, remember and recognize our human kinship with the Southern segregationist, as we remember and recognize our kinship with the Negro. We, too, are irrational, in our own individual ways. The North is ahead of the South in race relations only in that segregation is not imbedded in the structure of the laws, and police power is not used in favor of one side or the other. These are important differences, to be sure; but they are not important enough for the North to assume a moral superiority over the South.

Most of the people I know in the big cities of the North would never consider sending their children to the public schools. They maintain that it is a matter of educational quality; but emotionally it is because they do not want their children to go to school with Negroes and Puerto Ricans. The alternative of the private school for the middle- and upper-class white children of the South does not, in the main, exist. My New York friends assume that *my* children are not involved in the consideration of school integration, that as a matter of course they would not attend the public schools anyway. This, too, is irrationalism.

The consideration of public school integration involves wider questions than the rightness or the wrongness of it. It is a fact of life that, under the present circumstances, in certain places, the diehard segregationists will react with violence against an attempt at integration. Even a man of principle would hesitate to send his children into an area of potential violence, would hesitate to expose his children to the threat of mutilation that is often telephoned anonymously to parents in order to maintain a school boycott.

That such a situation could even exist is deplorable in the extreme; but pious assertions will not remove the reality. This does not mean that school integration must be delayed indefinitely because of the threat of violence; but it does mean that the pressures must be applied with sublety and intelligence, not blindly and arrogantly.

It is irrational to be selective in determining worthy objects of compassion or indignation. Yet often, in the North, I have seen newspapers or individuals become greatly exercised over a Southern Negro whose rights as an individual or as an American have been maltreated; and indeed they should be exercised. But at the same time I have seen the similar plight of a Southern white completely ignored.

Actually, in recent years, more whites than Negroes have been taken out of their homes and beaten by night riders. Recently in Alabama a white man was abducted and beaten, with the tragic result that he had to be committed to the State Hospital for the Insane. In another town, a white woman was taken out of her house and beaten—taken by mistake for another woman—and, though the police caught the assailants while she was still in their car, so their identity was widely known, no one was ever prosecuted. Neither of these flagrant cases aroused a perceptible degree of indignation or compassion in the North.

I believe that human dignity is the key. Wherever and whenever an assault on human dignity occurs, perpetrated by anyone on any individual, white or black, there is a diminishment of us all. We cannot be selective in compassion and understanding. We must rise up, as human beings, whether the individual involved fits into our current preconceptions or not. When any man, anywhere, is taken out of his home and flogged by masked men, so are we all flogged in our human spirit, whether the man be white or black, moral or immoral.

Yes. Human dignity. Our individual right to be individuals, regardless of race, color, or creed. If we remember this, if we feel this, if we believe this, in the deepest part of ourselves, we can forget about the color of a man's skin. The die-hard segregationist will deny the humanity of the Negro, though it is not rational to do so. The fanatic integrationist will deny the humanity of the white segregationist; it is equally irrational. Between the two extremes stand the men of good will, the men who try to understand and be compassionate, the men who recognize the shadow side of irrationality and prejudice within themselves and within others. Though we must never yield to irrationality, but instead endeavor to expose it to the control of consciousness, we must recognize its power in the human heart.

Though I fear that the battle will never be won on this level, I am definitely optimistic about the particular racial problem of the South. I believe that the Negro will within our lifetimes win a limited victory, in that segregation will be removed from the structure of our laws; in that, eventually, the police power will no longer be used on the side of the mob. And adjustment will be made that nearly every man will be able to accommodate within himself.

There are many good signs that this is coming to pass. The actions of the Governor of Georgia and the officials of the University of Georgia in effecting a token integration of their university was especially heartening. They demonstrated that indeed violence can be thwarted if the will to do so exists. The lawyer for a group of night-riders coming up for trial in an Alabama town asked the judge for a change of venue because local opinion would prejudice their case. This is highly indicative, since the night-riders have always relied on public opinion for their immunity.

There are also signs of loss, minor but always poignant. The Negroes in the South no longer sing, as they used to sing, with the full-throated joy that a white man can only envy. Even in the North, many professional Negro singers have studiously erased the lovely Negro musical quality from their voices, as though they were ashamed of their heritage. This, too, is a denial of individuality.

The demand upon us all is great. It is greatest of all, perhaps, upon the Negro race, for the crusade upon which they have embarked demands that each individual Negro bear the whole burden of his race, that each of them stand alone, individually, for the totality of his people. The failure of the individual, whether in anger or crime or rationality, becomes inevitably the failure of the race. And this is a terrible thing.

The white minority of the South, equally, bears the burden of humanity. Extremism is the denial of humanity. When forces clash darkly by night upon the plains of irrationality, then mankind must rise above itself to win the light of reason.

But I am hopeful. Hopeful, even, to the extent that perhaps, some day in the distant future, the sign on the highway outside my Southern town will be removed forever.

FAREWELL

TO THE CIVIL WAR

(*A Confession*)

Paul Green . . .

Playwright, novelist, poet, short story writer, essayist, teacher, screen scenarist; born on a farm near Lillington, North Carolina (where the life he knew was "much the same as that of his ancestors. On his father's farm he and his brothers worked the cotton and corn and cut timber shoulder to shoulder with the Negro laborers. Here his imagination fed on the beauty and loneliness of the wide fields and sky, the ever-changing life of the wooded swamps and hills, and the pathos and humor of the Negroes and the fervid poorer whites"); alumnus of the University of North Carolina where he studied playwriting under Professor Frederick H. Koch of the Carolina Playmakers; taught philosophy and dramatic art, turning more and more to writing as a career; published two volumes of one-act plays for the Negro Theater; won the Pulitzer prize for his long play *In Abraham's Bosom*; wrote other plays for New York production (*The Field God, The House of Connelly, Johnson, Roll Sweet Chariot*); wrote three volumes of short stories (*Wide Fields, Salvation on a String, Dog on the Sun*); three books of essays (*Dramatic Heritage, Drama and the Weather, The Hawthorn Tree*); two novels (*The Laughing Pioneer* and *This Body the Earth*); and *The Lost Colony* (first of the outdoor symphonic dramas that have spread into a movement in the South and elsewhere), followed by *The Common Glory, The Stephen Foster Story*, and numerous others.

To start with let me say I am tired of sectionalism, of regionalism—of cutting the nation up in parts and differentiating the one from the other and therefore the one against the other.

In short I am tired of the subject of the South—whether it's the Old South, the New South, the agrarian South, the industrial South, the boll-weevil South, the pellagra South, the Bible Belt South, the hookworm South, the corn-pone South, the one-gallus South, the Anglo-Saxon purity South, the peckerwood South, or even the emerging South.

I am tired too of hearing about the Southern Negro as an object of anguish and concern. The issue of segregation is settled. The principle of equality is established and living, and only an old corpse waits to be buried. There will be some wrangling of course over the disposition of the hulk, but it will soon fade away.

I am tired of both integration and segregation then. I'd like to be left alone to do some thinking about people as just people and forget color, except perhaps to remember that the blood of us all is red.

And as for the soul of man, it has no color at all. I've known that since a child—since the time I used to roll and tumble with the little Negro boys—my playmates and sworn buddies —on my father's farm.

I am tired too of the misshapen fiction characters who moan their wails and woes in the long-winded pages of what is called the Southern literary renaissance. In my present low mood at the fallen prestige of American idealism in the world, these characters seem to me as sorry and untruthful representatives of the human life they are supposed to represent as the old magnolia, honeysuckle, crinoline, roses, and mockingbird folks of a hundred years ago. True they're not as empty-headed, but since they are stuffed with their own excrement they give off a viler odor.

Now the Newer Criticism in England and America, to make a pertinent side reference, has its affection for spiders and the wasteland of dead hopes and dry bones. I know that. And it has long ago decided that it is a sorry business to be born into this world. So it is no surprise that the critics of this group find in the literature of the Southern renaissance a great affirmation for their sort of moral order and stability of the universe as well as their justification of man's wilful ways to God. It is no surprise, I say, that they find their affirmation in this literature of Freudian whining, in these case studies of sick and perverted Southern characters. But you and I who sweat in the collar and pay taxes should not be misled.

And I guess I'm tiredest of all of the subject of the Civil War. We've long had enough of it. But here it is with us and heaped up upon us through 1965, according to an act of Congress. So I guess there's no escape from talking about it. Maybe some of the talk will make sense.

The truth is, by any sane standard of reason and truth in these world-troubled days, this was one of the most senseless and unnecessary wars ever fought, Winston Churchill and others to the contrary. All wars of mankind's killing and cutting of throats are to me stupid and senseless, yes, but this one was a high mark of human foolishness.

Once it was under way, then of course the piteously heroic and epic and sublime things, as well as the petty, mean, silly, cynical, perverse, beastly, and tragic things that did happen would have to happen—or at least things of a similar kind— even from General Lee's falling on his knees night and morning asking help of Almighty God in the sky to General Grant's sucking on his bottle of monkey rum during these same hours here below to get aid for his side. (I guess I'd better not consider the irony, even blasphemously so, of which turned out to be the stronger help, or I'd be sunk and could go no further in writing this piece, since I'd have crossed orthodox civilization out of the book of my universe.)

I continue.

The fact that there were reasons for that war, which the historians prove in plenty, does not mean that it had to happen, that it had to *be* before it started to be. No. For there were other reasons which if put to work in time would have prevented it—the best of reasons being the use of common sense and self-control. But during those thirty or forty years of the early nineteenth century in which the nation stewed and boiled toward the catastrophe, rationality and common sense were absorbed into a wild and staggering sectional fervency —similar to the fervent nationalisms and party spirits elsewhere now threatening the world with another hideous war —this time a nuclear and blackout one.

And this sectionalism too had its cause. It came out of the exciting adventure of materialism. We can well call it materialism. In the taming of the new country the inventive genius of our people flourished, and the splurge of building and creating things—tools, engines, bridges, canals, roads, fields, schools, churches, cities, etc., etc.—this splurge of human activity for the subduing and the processing of nature, for the overpowering and shaping and directing of the natural environment all around and about, beat in the people's blood and took them wholly. And from long concentrating on these things they lost their perspective on other matters of importance and so grew enslaved to this materialism.

And so the adventure now of barter and trade and gambling

in physical commodities absorbed them, even to a stepped-up dealing in human flesh on the Southern auction block.

Thus in the common greed for these material creations and spoils in the new land, the heritage of our idealism faded and grew obscure. The dream of the founding fathers was pretty much lost sight of, and its once powerful categorical imperative of national virtue fell on deaf ears. Our democracy, created and documented in imagination and spiritual vision and based on the belief that the real values of life, the values that come first, are those of human character and manly worth and should apply equally to the nation and to the individuals in that nation—this democracy more and more surrendered its concept of values, of principle, to these other values, of business, of commerce, of the market place and the dollar. These became for the majority of the people and their leaders the finalities of life and the nation's primary purpose and aim. Everybody was doing it.

Of course in the days of the founding fathers there was plenty of gambling and spiritual waste, but we mustn't forget that it was in those days that the vision was created, was derived, was handed on to us.

Yes, as a people we lost sight of the American dream. We quit dreaming it. We forgot the truths put down in that vital Virginia Declaration of Rights of June 17, 1776. We forgot the Declaration of Independence. We forgot the great statement of social reality imbedded in the Constitution for us as citizens to live by. We continued to pay them lip service, true, but we had forgot them in our hearts. To repeat, we had gone hog-wild over the manipulation and creation and controlling of things—of building and ever building, building bigger and better, saying these things were better because they were bigger—and never stopping to ask for what purpose this great splurge of gross human activity was boiling up nor why the far reaches of the continent were being so energized.

So through the years the light of our leadership weakened and finally scales covered the eyes of the loud-mouthed ones in the market places and in the halls of government. What a pity no moral power was available to keep them dumb as they were sightless. But there was no such power available, and the more they shouted out their selfish sectional platitudes and prejudices, the more the nation went astray.

I tell the woeful tale as I feel it in my heart to be and so speak in defense of the dead.

So it was that more and more the engineer and inventor occupied the place of the statesman and the sage and more and more the salesman and the gambler took over the prescriptives of the educator and honest businessman, rather than less and less as had been intended. Sectionalism developed like a wild growth, and the welfare of the part took precedence over the welfare of the whole. The nation headed toward ruin.

And in their blindness the people began to quarrel more viciously than ever over the spoils of life. And why not, since they considered these spoils, these material things with their deeds of trust and registered promises in the courthouse, the most important matters between their birth and their death. And so in grabbing for them they fell afoul of one another's greedy reaching arms. So rights and responsibilities got confused with privilege and possessions and happiness became all tangled with duty. As I say, the vision was lost.

In these turmoilings and stirrings of misunderstandings and suspicion, then, the country broke itself into two parts, the North and the South. And bitterness surged into hate and fear, the one for the other.

And the same old story of man's folly and his pain was to be reenacted: war!

Arming themselves now, they put on contrasting uniforms to certify friend or foe so that the right sort of killing could take place—as is always the logic and custom in such upsurgings. And so they went at the business of murdering and destroying one another, and not only that but of destroying the very things which shortly before they had been so avid for and had quarreled about—slaves, boundaries, states rights, tariffs, railroads, shops, stores, churches, cotton, wheat, corn, factories, mines, goods, naval stores, etc., etc.

The blood-letting, the burning, the degradation, the muck and the misery that followed were incredible. For four long red scourgeful years the madness raged. And ever the people sweated and toiled and prayed and moaned, and ever the young men kept dying and screaming on the battlefields—and screaming as they died. The air was full of the usual whoopings-up and shibboleths of honor and of epic and tragic glory both, as the people and their sightless politicians urged themselves on.

And the grieving piteous Southern women hurried hither and yon and helped and healed as best as they could and wrung their twisted hands and wept. And in the wild black nights they loved their men even the more passionately so as to create more sons and daughters in a multitude who would go forth to fill the gaping ranks and devouring needs of war. And they blessed whatever pangs of birth might be which they could happily endure for so grand a cause.

But madness like a flaming meteor must finally burn itself out.

At last overcome by superior forces the South gave up—she called "Calf rope, enough! Peace—it is wonderful." The

North insisted that her enemy sister say "Uncle" and say it twice. Shamefully she had to, she said, and she did. The shooting stopped, but not the confusion and the misunderstanding, the sectionalism and the hate.

Much of these and their starveling-minded by-products continue to this day.

And have we as a people really learned anything from that dreadful slaughter?

Sometimes I doubt it, especially when I look around me now and see the kind of antics and posed parades and speakings and legislative appropriations and re-enactments and celebrations that are taking place in these Civil War centennial years.

My native state of North Carolina, for instance, has created by legislative enactment her own Confederate Centennial Commission and with generous financial support from the taxpayers' money to promote it. A Confederate Centennial!

Instead of prayers and laments and pleadings for forgiveness and solemn rememberings of that terrible civil strife in which seven hundred thousand young men ended their lives on earth, we have substituted a trade fair or even carnival spirit, with the old greed of buy and barter riding high like a death's head clown in the midst of it. Tourism is the ballyhoo with its folding money for gasoline and food and lodging and trinket and gew-gaw emblems of a bloody and inglorious past. Thousands and thousands come to attend these occasions, and business is booming. See the complacent smiles of the Commerce Department.

Virginia is far ahead of all other states in her harvest of tourist dollars, for she has more Civil War shrines for people to visit than any other. Her ground was reddened with more young men's blood than any other state. So now finally the tens of thousands of dead boys sleeping rotten in her soil find

their vindication and proof of the Southern demagogue's ring-
ing phrase "that they did not die in vain."

They're paying off now.

Consider the Virginia re-enactment some time ago of the
battle of Manassas. Bleachers were put up, chairs were brought
in by the wagonload, and seats were sold to the public at
prices ranging from $2.50 to $4.00. And the hordes of the
sons and daughters of Democracy Going Down came to witness the spectacle as if coming to a football game.

There was little that poor sensitive John Doe could do in
protest to that cynical farce. But I for one in my narrow
writing den did put up a hot and bilious prayer to my pagan
icon that the chiggers and seed ticks would be especially
numerous and hungry in the fields and woods of Manassas on
that July anniversary day and would attack the generals and
colonels and other officers and work havoc among them and
their privates inclusively, not forgetting to keep their little
stinging probes and augers all stiffened and burning for attack upon the foolish spectators.

Maybe my prayer did some good, for I read in the papers
the next day that at least one general fell off his horse (General Stonewall Jackson it was from Lenox, Massachusetts),
and other officers and enlisted men went wandering and
astray in the woods during the "exercises." Many a one "died"
in the wrong place, too, unseen, unwept, unhonored, unsung,
but not unstung. Maybe their bodily discomfort made them
forget their mimeographed instructions as to just what to do
on the field of valor, and so they got all gummed up.

How about that? How crazy can we get? Answer: crazy
enough to start building fallout shelters and arming them
against our neighbors. Crazy enough to continue manufactur-
ing nuclear bombs twenty-four hours a day, when already

we've got enough (Russia has too) to destroy the entire world. Again a madness on top of madness—and not the madness of a war one hundred years ago, but madness now, in helping prepare the proper psychology and the means for another possible war to come.

But one madness tends to breed another. There is a connection.

Some say the nation was finally unified and born out of that Civil War and that we became one people because of it and we could have become so in no other way. My kindly poet neighbor from the slabs of the sunburnt West says that before the war the United States required a plural verb "are" but after the war the plural became the singular "is." At last we were one nation and the war made us one. And the scholars—many of them—also say this was a movement in history, a gathering of mysterious and opposing forces in the long stretches of time. The war was fated to happen, and the poor human beings concerned were the playthings of fate. There was nothing they could do to stop it.

Oh no, no, no! I don't believe it for a moment and can't believe it.

This is the old *post hoc ergo propter hoc* reasoning that seeks to justify the event after it has taken place, which seeks to justify the unjustifiable. And it's all bassackwards. The way to life is not death, the way to unity is not disunity, the way to love is not hate. If this is so then only madness is reasonable and man's existence is the same as nonexistence, a nothing, not even a whiff of gas in the monstrous galaxy of gas.

But man exists. Joy can be experienced, pain can be felt; self-consciousness, self-awareness, is a fact. Man knows he is, and as he knows, he knows he has the power of choice and of hope. And that means self-freedom and self-responsibility. Given that, the imperative to righteous action follows.

A misguided people made that war. And the misguidance was of their own doing. They and they only were to blame. And why were they misguided? As I said above, in greed they lost their vision.

A nation can commit sin and go down to damnation the same as a man. There is no moral safety in numbers.

And what misguidance, what sin are we up to now? Let us think on this, let us search our hearts, yea, the while we think of the lost dead and the funeral pyres of hopes-in-ashes around the earth and the vicious monstrous chance that more innocent millions of men, women, and children (weep for Hiroshima, for Nagasaki and American shame!)—that more of these helpless ones will be shoveled purposeless and forever gone into the lightless ground.

We must be up and doing—up! up! Look ahead, ahead!

And for me, the North and the South played the fool back a hundred years ago. That fight was a piece of witless folly. That sums it up for me, and I am ready to write it out of my concerning, ready to turn my back on it, to forget it.

For now the matters of concern before us are bigger than any sectionalism, bigger than any regionalism, bigger than any North or South or any one nation for that matter. They are of global size—the machine and technological age makes it a fact—and they can only be handled in terms of the globe.

The Old South and the Civil War have been mulled over, toiled over, moiled over, kneaded and re-kneaded, interpreted and reinterpreted to the limit of human endurance. And I declare here for myself that there is no light, no message of hope, no living truth to be found in them and their doings that

will—as the Southern Regional Council recently suggested—
"strengthen us for the future," that will help us "to play our
part in the world today"—except the truth by omission, of
negation and denial, the truth that the old South was an error
in history and the Civil War was the horror resulting from
that error.

And what do you do with an error? Put it behind you. And
Humphy Dumpty from the wall? Leave him busted where he
lies.

But if we jump over the old South and go back to the
eighteenth century and the founding fathers—"neither North
nor South"—that's something else. There we find light, hope,
truth, and help for the present age, help in our heritage, help
for preventing another kind of Civil War, this time a world
Civil War. And the challenge before us now is to be busy at
once with all our soul and energy in putting that help to work.

Visualize George Washington and Thomas Jefferson against
John C. Calhoun and Jefferson Davis as examples of statesmanship, of forces of world influence, of sources of strength
for the needs of the present world, and you will see what I
mean.

No, there is no salvation to be got now from digging in the
sodden dunghill of the Old South and the Civil War. Let's
forget them, or if we must remember, then remember them
for what they were, for their sins and errors, and so keep
before us the stern warning of their failures, their perversions,
and their death as we work on toward the days of humanity's
triumph and of life ahead.

For now our business is world business, a united world
business, and it is urgent!

RED ROSES
AND REDSTONES

Hoke Norris . . .

Literary critic of *The Chicago Sun-Times;* native of North Carolina, former reporter for *Elizabeth City Daily Advance, News and Observer,* Winston-Salem *Journal,* and Associated Press; Nieman Fellow at Harvard University, 1950-51; captain in combat intelligence, Army Air Forces, in Southwest Pacific Theater, during World War II; author of a score of short stories and a novel, *All The Kingdoms of Earth.*

Who knows the South? One must ask, Which South? There are many Souths. Each knows his own. I know two Souths. I know my South, an old South of childhood and youth, and now, without quite believing or understanding, a new South. This new South I saw during a summer trip I took through Alabama, Tennessee, Georgia, and North Carolina. On this long road I learned that when a Southerner goes home again these days, he goes with longing and uncertainty, and a new fear.

He goes remembering his South. He goes remembering Jersey cows cropping grass in a green valley beside still waters, he goes remembering red roses growing on red ditchbanks,

Reprinted by special permission of *The Chicago Sun-Times.*

and the Negro kids he fought with because their path to school crossed his, and remembering the gravestones of his forefathers, and the odors of magnolia in bloom and barbecue cooking on an open pit, the feel of the earth and the grass beneath his feet when he could start going barefooted again in the spring, the tug of a catfish upon a cotton twine, the cry of the whippoorwill in the cool of the evening and the long, far call of the dove in the cool of the morning, and the winds that blew down the crops and the rattle of the hail that destroyed them and the sun that revived them, the rustle of leaves in autumn chill and the smell of their burning, and a life full of honeyed words and two races living apart and never questioning their separation and their alienation, and a quietness and a peace that children everywhere think will never end.

But he remembers, too, this home-fearing, homeward-yearning Southerner, the rest of his South. He remembers a refusal to shake hands with a Negro, long ago on a porch grown with morning glories, a black hand flicking slightly forward, instinctively perhaps, in greeting, and then withdrawn, and a darkness flashing across a black face, and then gone. This is remembered shame, never forgotten. But he remembers awakenings too. He remembers his father—never one to mix the races, but a Baptist preacher and a good man who would permit no degradation of any human being in his presence—reproving an unthinking, slanderous remark about a colored woman, "Don't you say that, don't you ever say that." This was the beginning of awakening, though unrecognized at the time. He remembers a joke he told—a Mandy and Rastus joke—and a thoughtful friend who did not laugh, who asked instead, "Would it be funny if you told it about white folks?" It would not have been funny, and this

too was an awakening. And he remembers the Army, and the
doors marked "Officers Only," refused to him because he was
a private. Now he knew that he despised segregation; he
would cut his throat before he would live like this for the
rest of his life; yet many were segregated for all their days
upon earth. This was awakening, perhaps the final awakening.
Never again would he feel quite the same about his South.
Yet he could not forsake it or cease to love it, remembering
the earth and the grass beneath the soles of his feet, the catfish, the red roses on red ditchbanks, the whippoorwill and
the dove, and the gravestones of his ancestors. He would always remember.

But now he remembers, too, this Southerner returning after
years of absence, that history has at last caught up with the
Southland. He knows—intellectually, but perhaps not emotionally yet—that the wave that is carrying the African in
Africa to freedom is the same wave that will carry the African
in America to freedom. He cannot believe that it will be swept
back into the sea of colonialism and paternalism by any pitiful
broom that any white man can devise. Yet the thing has happened so fast, so quickly, and the voices he has heard from the
South have been so loud and angry and the acts of his fellow
white man as he has learned of them from afar have been so
violent and irrational, the stirring of the Negroes so sudden
and implacable, so determined and yet so peaceful and un-
resisting, in the desegregation of the schools, in sit-ins, in
riding buses for freedom—all in its apparent abruptness has
perplexed and even frightened him. What does this home-
ward-going Southerner find now in this old home of his?

I went home to the South in company with a friend from
Chicago. We went on business. But the Freedom Riders had
just passed through. "You're here because of them, aren't

you?" the Southerners asked us, always, eventually, and we were off—off in the inevitable talk about The Question, The Problem. We couldn't get away from it. If you go South these days, you travel in a morass of controversy and perplexity. The Southerners want to talk about it; apparently they welcome a stranger for the opportunity he gives them to talk their hearts out. Maybe they can't talk among themselves, or think they can't. Sometimes unpleasant things do happen to people who talk too much, in the South as everywhere else.

Our first stop was Atlanta, an hour and a half from Chicago by jet. On the approach to the airport we saw roads growing through the red earth like angry wounds (no red roses here), and a cloverleaf interchange that might have been Chicago's, or New York's, or San Francisco's. The airport was a new one; it looked much like San Francisco's, or Idlewild, or like O'Hare if they ever finish it. This was our first lesson: The New South is beginning to look like the New North. We entered the airport. Confederate flags were on sale at the newsstand. But Negro boys mingled with white boys in a group of traveling students; Negroes were being served by white waitresses at the lunch counter (this was *Atlanta?*); and the *Atlanta Journal*, which covers Dixie and much of the rest of the world like the dew, bannered racial violence in South Africa, and on the same front page detailed the steps being taken to desegregate Atlanta schools and to clean up the ugly mess left by mobs in Birmingham and Montgomery.

Birmingham, Alabama, was our destination. We left Atlanta and in a few minutes flew over a brood of lights nested in the darkness of velvet Southern night. That was Anniston, Alabama, down there. Down there somewhere, perhaps, oddly, almost unbelievably, were men who a few days before has slashed the tires of a bus and set it afire because they disapproved of its passengers. How could this be, in a night so still and tender? And what would those men of violence be doing now? What would they be saying and thinking? I hadn't the faintest idea. Yet I reflected that they were probably men with families they loved and jobs they were faithful to, men who did their stern duty as they saw it. That they were dreadfully and tragically misled and deluded was their dreadful tragedy and delusion, and the South's.

Already I was perturbed by The Question. I turned through the pages of the *Atlanta Journal,* seeking other news. On page 26, I read that Faith Forrester had married William Gallatin Baker, Jr., and that they would live in New York. On page 37, I read that George Dewey Bankston, a retired Atlanta postman and winner of the Purple Heart during the First World War, had died while visiting his son. Come Freedom Riders, come buses made torches, come lead pipes and red blood at bus stations, the functions and the joys and the sorrows of life and living never cease, anywhere.

Birmingham, we found, had an old, small airport, but was building a new one. I imagined that it would look like Atlanta's. Southern-raised though I was, I was not prepared for the soft, concerned voice of the man who would drive the airport limousine into the city—a voice from which all the internal R's and final G's had been bred long ago. "What paht of town you all goin' to?" he asked. We felt that he really cared.

He drove us toward the city in night, country dark, through the smells of smoke and forest, past a cemetery that in red neon offered Perpetual Care, and a flaming smokestack at Hayes aircraft, and small factories and small homes. Our driver talked with a woman passenger returning home after a visit to Atlanta. "Had any more trouble here?" she asked. "No, thank God," the driver said, with genuine thanksgiving.

They discussed the weather. It had been sort of warm. Got up to almost 80 during the afternoon.

The driver left us at the Pick-Bankhead Hotel, an ancient edifice which to the people of Birmingham is still the Bankhead, a name renowned in American politics and in American entertainment. In our rooms we turned on the television sets. There would be an election for mayor the next day, and one candidate, Tom King, was on the screens, disclaiming NAACP support, deploring outside interference by radicals and federal marshals in the affairs of Alabama, and declaring himself a segregationist. (We were told later that he was considered the local liberal. He lost the election.) Before retiring, my friend and I strolled the streets of Birmingham. They were almost deserted. Sounds were muted and slow. The two bus stations, Greyhound and Trailways, seemed innocent and placid after their storms. The races weren't mixing in the waiting rooms. We walked back to the hotel. A full moon was shining on the city, the same moon you may have seen that night, wherever you were. It shone alike on the the just and the unjust, the colored and the white.

The next morning, as it happened, the first business I transacted was with an old Negro man sitting on the edge of the lawn of the First Presbyterian Church of Birmingham, Alabama. I bought a bag of peanuts from him. He said that business was good. So were the peanuts.

And the first white man I talked to, as it turned out, was a Roman Catholic priest, just down the hot street from the Presbyterians. Years ago, he told me, he had come from Ireland, a volunteer for service in the Mobile-Birmingham Diocese—a missionary diocese, deep in the Deep South, in the Heart of Dixie, as the Alabama license plates proclaim it.

He was still here, still talking in an Irish brogue. A year before the school desegregation decision of 1954, he told me, the diocese had quietly desegregated Spring Hill College, a liberal arts institution run by the Jesuits in Mobile. The Negro students just showed up there, he said, and nothing happened except that a few white contributors may have decided not to contribute any more. "They keep no records of race on the registrations, and they honestly can't tell you how many Negroes they have," he said. "The students aren't guinea pigs. They're men and women. They're there to get an education."

The diocese now has 115,000 members, 15,000 of them Negroes, in Alabama and northwest Florida, he said, and it's growing at the rate of about 1,300 conversions and 3,000 to 4,000 infant baptisms a year; seventy priests work among Negroes and the diocese operates thirty schools for Negroes. "We haven't desegregated the schools," he said. "The schools are built on an area basis, and residential segregation establishes school segregation, though white priests and nuns teach at the schools. In Birmingham, Mobile, and Montgomery we have hospitals where Negro doctors can treat their own patients. But no—we haven't made any grandiose statements about desegregation. We try to do the best we can within the pattern of state law. The schools must observe state law or they can close them down. That's a constant threat here."

I went my way, musing about how scarce Catholics had been in the South that I had known. I had a talk a little later with the pastor of one of the largest Protestant churches in Birmingham. He was a young man, busy and dedicated, as the Catholic priest had been, and I did not keep him long. But I did ask, "What could a white Southern pastor tell his white Southern congregation on the Sunday after that mob violence at the bus station?" He thought for a moment. It must have been a troubling question. "We haven't taken any position for or against segregation or desegregation," he said at last. "But we have always opposed violence. On that Sunday I told them of the need for baptism by the Holy Spirit, and that until we have that we're going to experience trouble. It was Pentecostal Sunday and we—the other pastors and I—used that occasion to tell them this."

There was another minister, a visitor from another Southern city, to whom I repeated a complaint that I had heard: That the Birmingham clergy was not offering leadership for what was bound to come in the South. The minister smiled, rather wistfully, I thought. "It is true," he said, "that my church has no Negro members, but I'm getting a little tired of hearing that 11 o'clock Sunday morning is the most segregated hour in America. I'm not sure whether that saying is relevant. A Negro would be welcome in my church, but I'd have to tell him that he'd have to be willing to take what he'd have to put up with. We haven't had any Negroes apply for membership. But I will say this," he went on, "that while it is bad for outsiders to make trouble, the Freedom Riders may have done one good thing. They may have stirred up the people, the leaders, and made them realize that plans have got to be made for what's coming, if they're to avoid violence."

And then, later in the day, there was a handsome Southern lady with honey in her voice. She stood at the edge of her garden. "They're moss roses," she said, pointing. "They say that if this red dirt of ours will grow anything, it'll grow roses. And it does. You see roses everywhere, don't you?" In a few minutes: "You're here because those Freedom Riders came through, aren't you? Let me tell you something," she went on, squaring her shoulders, *"The New York Times* wrote that fear is stalking the streets of Birmingham. Have you seen any fear here?"

My friend and I acknowledged that all did seem quiet.

"Yes, it is quiet here," she said (magnolias bloomed behind her, and the tiny roses swayed in the breeze). "And that's the worst thing, the most untrue thing, that's ever been said about us. Why, we've got good Negroes here, and we love them and they love us, but we want them in their place and they want us in our place. It works both ways. Why, I love my maid, and the man who works in the yard here. When he got in trouble, through no fault of his and I knew it wasn't, we stood by him. That's the way it is. They're good people and they want their own churches and their own schools, where they can take part in things. We don't want to share our lunch counters with them, or our rest rooms or our schools, and we won't. And they don't want to."

She looked to us for reply but we had not come to argue.

"Would you want your daughter to marry one?" she asked, inclining her head in the warm, bright sunlight. "Would you?"

And, still later, an executive in a labor union: "I used to work in a foundry beside a Negro man who'd been there 10 years longer than I had. He could work rings around me. And he got 10 cents an hour less than I did. Was that right? No, it wasn't, and in most places now they get equal pay for equal work, like it ought to be. But they still don't get a chance at training, and unless they're trained, how're they going to get jobs that pay? As for segregation—I'll tell you what Phil Murray said once. He said that the union had a policy, a policy against segregation, but he knew that we had a situation down here. We do. So we segregate our locals, and we have separate drinking fountains for white and colored. We don't want to tear up our locals over this thing. We want first to build the union, not tear it down. The trouble is that the Klan and the White Citizens' Council infiltrate the locals. They get in before you know it, and then to get rid of them you'd have to tear up your locals."

He shook his head. He didn't have the answer.

Nor did a professional man I had lunch with. "They just don't know what they're asking," he said, in soft, Southern exasperation. "They're asking us to change ways that've been unchanged for a hundred years. Why, it's just a question of who's going to rule. The white people in the counties that have Negro majorities just don't want Negro mayors and legislators. It's the same in Chicago, and you know it is, though you're hypocritical about it up there. I've been to Chicago many times and I know it pretty well. Would your white folks want a Negro mayor? And look at what happens when they threaten to move in—look at what happened at Deerfield. And walk north on Michigan Avenue, above the bridge. The only Negro you see up there is holding a door open for you. No—I can't see that you're making any progress there at all.

"But we are making progress, or were, before all this came along. All this has stiffened resistance, but even so, we're still making progress. Did you know that the municipal golf course in Mobile had been integrated? Three or four Negro foursomes showed up there and nothing happened. It was done quietly. It was like the clerks waiting on customers in the stores. They used to always leave a Negro to go wait on a white person. They were following custom, and the Negro didn't have any money, anyway. Then suddenly I realized one day that the clerks weren't doing that any more. They were taking customers first-come, first-served. One reason, I suppose, was that the Negro began having money, and he might take it elsewhere.

"And the elevators. They used to be segregated. Then one day suddenly I realized that they weren't segregated any more. I made some inquiries, and found out that at the Frank Nelson Building there was a lawyer who had a lot of Negro clients. After court, they'd come back and he'd have to go to his office by one elevator, his clients by another. He found it inconvenient and maybe embarrassing, and one day he spoke to the building superintendent about it, and he just took the signs down without saying anything about it, and nothing happened.

"But now—all that's happened has stiffened resistance. Yet I will say this—those were outsiders the other day at the bus station, both the Freedom Riders and the mob. I heard that one white man over there had been seen at the Autherine Lucy trouble at the University of Alabama, stirring up trouble. But the politicians still can't win an election without preaching segregation—they just can't. Outside interference has stiffened the opposition, and while most people don't like violence, and some know that change has got to come, you've still got politics, you know. And communications—they've broken down completely between the races, and nobody can advocate communication—he'd be afraid of being called soft on desegregation. So we just don't talk to each other any more. There used to be delegations of Negroes to city hall, to make their requests. I don't remember when there was ever a delegation at city hall."

"Communication?" cried a Negro leader in his segregated office building. "Communication? At city hall? You went there and you begged. It was always servant and master. The only real communication is at the ballot box. That's where we can cut 'em off if we don't like what they're doing. It isn't communication when I've got to call him mister and he calls me by my first name. There's never been any communication between us because it's always been master and servant between us. I communicate man to man, human being to human being.

"As for the Freedom Riders—they tell us we've got to have a cooling-off period. I'm not interested in cooling off or in heating up. I'm just interested in correcting injustice. They tell us it'll cause trouble. Trouble? Man, a Negro is born in trouble and lives in trouble all his life. Trouble isn't new to him."

We left his office and hailed a taxi driven by a Negro. He shook his head; he couldn't carry us; he would call a white cab for us. He called, and when the white driver arrived he handed the Negro a dime. Why this taxi segregation, we asked later, when the buses had been desegregated? Just custom, we were told.

In the evening we went to visit friends on Red Mountain. They had just recently moved to Birmingham from New York. We had drinks on their terrace, in the cool of dusk. The hills were violet. There, and later, at a restaurant, we talked The Question.

"It is a problem," the husband said. "You've got no idea how some Negroes live, whatever the reason they live that way. They aren't immoral. They're just unmoral. They live like animals. It'd be a blow to education, a bad one, to put them in classes with white children. Oh, I know that some people here wouldn't object strongly to desegregation, because they know it wouldn't affect them. But it would affect the middle and lower classes, and they're worried."

Out a window of the restaurant, on the horizon, we could see the flare of an open hearth at a steel mill. Nearby stood Vulcan, the iron statue on Red Mountain, which, according to local legend, sometimes waves to Electra, on top of the Alabama Power Company Building. Both statues carry torches. They burn red on days when there's been a fatality in an automobile accident. Birmingham is safety-conscious.

"With the people I know," the husband continued, "I've found that the old generation is bitter and strong for segregation, the middle generation accepts segregation, and the third, the young ones, don't really care. They're sensible enough to know that it won't really affect them."

"To change the subject," I began, cutting into my filet.

"Please do," my host said. We laughed together. "Sometimes I get terribly tired of The Problem."

Tired of it or not, it was a matter of the most imperative concern for a business leader we talked to the next day. He said that he knew change was coming; he even predicted that the medical school of the University of Alabama would admit Negro students, and would do so perhaps sooner than anybody expected. "They've got Chinese and Japanese there already," he said, "so why not Negroes?"

But he deplored the lack of leadership among the politicians and the clergymen, in Birmingham and elsewhere. And he spoke in some melancholy about the candidate who had won the election for mayor: "He's a good boy. He's not the kind to talk that way. But he had to, to get elected. One trouble here is that the people who own this town don't live in it. They live in the suburbs. They can't vote. If they could have voted, the other fellow might have won. But they're jolted up now, and so are the Negro leaders. They're scared to death of this tension, and they know that something's got to be done to prepare for what's coming, so there won't be violence. Nashville did it. Atlanta did it. Why can't Birmingham?"

He handed us a copy of a resolution adopted by the directors of the Birmingham Chamber of Commerce. "We did that after the Freedom Riders came to town," he said. "We should have done it before." The resolution requested various civic agencies to "enlarge their duties to include the study of means of creating better relations with all groups, regardless of their race or religion, to the end of promoting the civic, economic, industrial, and social welfare of the people of the Birmingham territory."

"This," our acquaintance said, "is the beginning of an attempt to go around the politicians. They can't get elected without tirading about segregation, but we can do something, we hope, by meeting with the Negro leaders and finding out what we can do to prepare for what's ahead."

And what is ahead?

We left our friend's office and walked out into the close, intimate, personal heat of the Southern sun. All about Birmingham the stacks of the steel mills were sending up smoke the color of burned orange; people were working, going to movies, getting married, spending money, dying. We took a white taxi back to the hotel. On the way we asked the driver what he thought was coming.

"Nothing," he said. "Not a thing's going to happen."

"But some of the leaders say they are, and they're going to help change them."

"The leaders? They won't be touched by this thing. Most of 'em live out of town, in the suburbs. They'll send their children to private schools. They do already. Who're they to tell us what to do?"

Back at the hotel, we read in the Southern papers column

after column of testimony about the violence at the bus stations—all the lead-pipe blood and gore of the thing—and we expressed admiration for the Southern papers that air this new Southern unpleasantness, that make no attempt to hide the ugly facts. Then we checked out of the Bankhead, rented a car, and set out northward, toward Huntsville, ninety miles away. The day was hot. Cows stood in the shade and chewed their cuds. Red roses bloomed on red ditchbanks. Tractors pulled plows in dusty fields. Just outside Huntsville we passed a 1947 Chevrolet sedan driven by a woman in a flowered pokebonnet. In a few minutes we drove past the Redstone Baptist Church, and the Redstone Motel, and approached the arsenal where man is assembling the materials and the devices that will some day take him to the moon, and beyond.

In Huntsville, during our spare time, we discussed what Birmingham had taught us. We had learned that the Freedom Riders, now come and gone, carrying their wounds and their cause to other cities, had left behind shock, dismay, and perplexity; that if they had accomplished nothing else at all, they had jolted Birmingham and possibly some other Southern cities into a realization that "something had to be done" to prepare for "what is to come." The interracial group in Birmingham was a first tentative groping for a way that would bring white and Negro together in an attempt to do what Nashville and Atlanta had done. That is, either prevent violence or, if it comes, end it, when another time of the test comes. And that time arrives in the South, of course, when some attempt is made to transform a Southern all-white facility of some sort into a "desegregated" facility. Our Birmingham friend had felt the absence of political leadership, which had just been demonstrated in the failure of authority at the bus stations, and so now the new race relations group, he had said, would "go around" the politicians toward the goal. He perhaps also recalled that the governor of Alabama had said recently about school desegregation, "If you think they've had trouble in New Orleans, just wait until they try integration here. There'll be hell to pay. . . . If the federal government continues in its present course, the only solution will be to close the schools. . . . I'll be one of the first ones stirring up trouble, any way I can."

Trouble? I asked an acquaintance in Huntsville, remembering the governor and our Birmingham experience. What kind of trouble?

He pondered for a moment, and then answered obliquely, "They just don't know what's happening to 'em."

"They? Who? And what is happening to 'em?"

"These people who can't think of anything but race. They've got a status that's based not on wealth or profession, or social or political position, but on the easiest status in the world, and yet the hardest. Status based on race alone. You don't have to do a thing to get it except be born. And if it's all you've got, poor and shabby though it is, you fight when it's threatened. It's threatened, and they're fighting, and they're losing, because it's a status that just can't survive attack."

But what these race-obsessed men and women—and Governor John Patterson among them—do not know or choose to ignore is that the desegregation of government and of public services and facilities has a long history in the South. Many Southern cities have had Negro policemen and firemen and aldermen for years, and gradually, through those years, the courts have chipped away at the "equal but separate" concept in both public schools and public transportation until it has completely vanished from the federal canon. It's as if the Supreme Court had been carefully, deliberately preparing the South for the decision of 1954 that declared the segregation of public schools unconstitutional. And through all those years, despite cries of havoc, despite forebodings of violence and bloodshed, many facilities have been thrown open to Negroes, and in most places nothing at all has happened except that white and colored began meeting where they had never met before. This is the story that has never penetrated the intelligence of the racists, just as it has never penetrated to the outside world.

When the facts are assembled, you learn that the longest record of desegregation has been made by the colleges, and universities. They began accepting Negro students long before the decision of 1954. Under court order, the University of Maryland desegregated in 1936, and the University of West Virginia did so voluntarily in 1938 and the universities of Delaware and Arkansas in 1946 (or just before Jackie Robinson went to work for the Dodgers). Some degree of desegregation in state universities and colleges, under pressure of court orders, followed in Oklahoma (1948), Kentucky (1949), Louisiana, Missouri, Texas, and Virginia (1950), North Carolina (1951), and Tennessee (1952). The District of Columbia voluntarily merged its two formerly one-race colleges into one college in 1954. Since then, state universities have been desegregated, under court order, in Florida (1958) and Georgia (1961); in Alabama, the university had its famous Negro co-ed Autherine Lucy for several days in 1956 but while under order to admit Negroes, it has not done so. (Alabama, however, does have two desegregated private colleges. One, Spring Hill College, in Mobile, is run by the Jesuits, who desegregated it in 1953, as I had been told by the Irish priest in

Birmingham. The other, Talladega College, in Talladega, is a Congregationalist Christian school whose charter, granted in 1867, opened it to all races. It is predominantly Negro and its numbers of white students have been small or nonexistent through the years. In 1961 it had one white student, one Indian, and one Nigerian, and a faculty of 29, about one third of it white.)

As for the public schools, it happened that there was one case of desegregation in the South even before the 1954 decision. Friona, in west Texas, admitted Negroes in 1953. Since then, some degree of desegregation (ranging from less than 1 per cent of Negroes in schools with whites to 84.1 per cent in the District of Columbia) has been inaugurated among public schools in all Southern states except Mississippi, Alabama, and South Carolina.

Georgia joined the majority after my visit in the summer of 1961. Atlanta desegregated the 11th and 12th grades of its schools in the autumn. The plan is gradually to effect desegregation thereafter a grade at the time, from the top downward. This is a reversal of the "Nashville plan," under which desegregation begins in the first grade and creeps upward, a grade at the time, through the years. There are, of course, other "plans" for desegregation: pupil assignment, free choice of schools by pupils, rigid district lines, local option. The Supreme Court has upheld some of them, voided others, depending on local conditions. This is part of the court's plan: within reason to fit the desegregation process to the temper of individual communities.

Though in his exasperated outburst our Birmingham friend may have considered Atlanta and Nashville as ideal examples for his city to follow, both have been the scene of racial tension and violence. In Nashville, reported a man long familiar with the story, John Kasper, the traveling disciple of racism, succeeded in recruiting considerable local help when the city desegregated its schools. "I think," my friend said, "that most of the crowds at the schools were just parents there to see how their children were faring, but rocks were thrown and epithets hurled about, and the police seemed undecided just what to do. I think that they were merely uncertain of their ground, unsure what to do. But then somebody bombed a school where one Negro pupil had enrolled, and the police really went to work. They blocked off the school areas, started arresting people, and went into federal court and got injunctions against Kasper and some other white men, and in twenty-four hours things had quieted down. That was the end of it."

This explanation, however, omits the subtleties of the Nashville situation, which my friend now provided: The city calls itself the "Athens of the South"—it boasts a replica of the Parthenon in a public park, a bustling cultural program that includes a fine symphony orchestra, and thirteen colleges and universities, including Vanderbilt. Its business community seems progressive and enlightened, and some civic organizations and clergymen adopted positions opposing violence. All this together, plus vigorous police action once it was prompted by violence, helped Nashville weather its storm.

Most of the statistics and chronology in the Southern desegregation process I obtained in Nashville at the headquarters of the Southern Education Reporting Service. This agency, composed in the main of former newspapermen, was organized by Southern leaders in journalism and education to do a complete and objective job of reporting on the South's school situation —a job it performs in excellent fashion. It is thoughtful and even philosophic about its job. For instance, it carefully distinguishes between the word "desegregation," by which it

means the mere mixing of the races, and the word "integration," by which it means community acceptance of that
mixing. It deals in more than abstract semantics when it does
so. There is a real difference: the difference between intellectual acceptance and emotional acceptance of desegregation,
and a nicety of language is required to make it clear. The man
who told me Nashville's story said to me, "I'm not going to
tell you that Nashville citizens are integrationist, but they're
willing to live with it."

Perhaps the same goal will be achieved in Atlanta, where a
start has already been made. That the city's record has been
good, and that it will probably remain so, is a blessing for
which Atlantans can thank their two newspapers, the *Journal*
and the *Constitution*, which through the years, in the midst of
Deep South tensions, have always counseled peaceful processes
and law observance; its strong, vigorous mayor, now retired,
William B. Hartsfield, and its chief of police, Herbert Jenkins;
and, oddly enough, the violence that erupted at the University
of Georgia, in Athens, in January, 1961.

One Atlantan told me this story, about the sit-ins in Atlanta,
which demonstrates the city at work on its problems:

"It was Saturday at Rich's, which is the biggest department
store in the Southeast, and Negroes with placards were parading on one side of the street, picketing the store, and the Klan
was parading on the other side of the street. There were cops
all about, and things kept on a pretty quiet level. But somebody heard one of the Klansmen say to another one, 'I sure
would like to get at them niggers over there.' 'Man, I would
too,' said the other one, 'but I hear the cops got dogs out here.'
And they probably did.

"But seriously, what happened was this: The day after
Thanksgiving, the Negro students blanketed the downtown

area with sit-ins—department, variety, and drug stores—every establishment where other parts of the business were open to their trade. The merchants closed the sat-upon facilities. The Negroes drifted away. Same thing the next day. Then the merchants closed down all eating facilities indefinitely. From that point, the Negroes' protest settled into boycott and picketing. Then came the Klan that Saturday afternoon to march around Rich's as a demonstration of support for the merchants' action in upholding segregation. You see their warped thinking? They came into downtown Atlanta to show the beleaguered merchants that there was somebody who was behind 'em, by God.

"Midway of the afternoon there arrived on the scene Lester Maddox, restaurateur, segregationist, candidate for mayor in 1955 and again this year, founder and president of Georgians Unwilling to Surrender—GUTS, or, if you prefer, GUS. Mr. Maddox fell into step with Grand Dragon Craig, and into earnest conversation, addressing the man in the sheet as 'Brother Craig.' Shortly thereafter, the Klan paraders withdrew. Was Mr. Maddox responsible, as he later claimed? Was he called into the breach by the merchants? We've never been certain, but my guess is yes to both questions.

"Here's the sequel, and another example, if belated, of Atlanta's good sense and good handling of these matters: This spring the president of the Chamber of Commerce, acting for the merchants and the elder statesmen among Negro leaders, announced the successful conclusion of negotiations: The Negroes would suspend demonstrations and boycotts, and the merchants would promise to desegregate eating facilities after school desegregation this fall."

During that fall, the eating places were peacefully desegregated, and Lester Maddox lost, by nearly two to one, in his second attempt to make himself mayor of Atlanta. The winner was Ivan Allen, Jr., a progressive businessman and a "moderate" in race relations. Maddox resorted to the usual epithets and alarums. He used the old words and terms—socialistic, communistic, NAACP. They just didn't work. Perhaps the overwhelming defeat of this race baiter can be attributed, in large part, to the two Atlanta papers, which opposed him all the way. In the *Journal*, a front-page columnist who calls himself Piney Woods wrote near the end of the campaign (and remember, this is one Southerner talking about another Southerner):

> My Grandpa used to have a mite inelegant but mighty expressive saying. "The dog has returned to his vomit." I thought about it for the first time in a long time when I read where Lester Maddox had opened his runoff campaign for mayor of Atlanta with a statement that the racial issue was the biggest one in the election. As you know, I am a stomp-down segregationist of long standing. But I've got enough sense to know nothing is going to be solved by tin-horn demagogues hollering "NIGGER, NIGGER!!" For the sake of peaceful race relations as well as the future of Atlanta, I hope the voters tell Lester to quit waving that bloody shirt and go back to his short-order skillet.

As for the University of Georgia and its role in the desegregation of public schools, my Atlanta friend explained: "The people of Georgia love their university with a love that passes all understanding unless you happen to be a Georgian. And when it seemed last winter for a while that they might close it, they were all shaken up about it. The thing started when two Negroes applied for admission and the courts said they were obviously being barred because of race and that the university had to admit them. The two students registered under tension, but without violence, and began classes. But then there was a student demonstration, and then a night later a riot.

The governor ordered the two students suspended and brought to Atlanta for safety.

"On the scene that night there were about eight characters from suburbs known to be Klan centers, and six or seven were identified as Klansmen. The police arrested the eight, and found that one of them owned a car loaded with weapons and ammunition. Why weren't the state patrolmen sent to Athens? Well—we've made a lot of guesses, none of the favorable to the politicians, but the patrolmen did finally get there. They took the two students to Atlanta. The next day a federal judge ordered them reinstated. The governor said then that it was a case of either close the university or obey the court, and the students re-entered under guard. The possibility that the university might be closed brought the politicians to their senses, or at least gave them an excuse to be sensible. The governor went to the legislature—it was quite a dramatic thing—and in effect asked the legislature to abolish massive resistance and give the state local option on whether to close the schools or not, and on how to desegregate if they wanted to. So Atlanta got its chance.

"The mayor and the chief are determined that there's to be no violence, and I think there won't be. The police are ready, and it's going to be hard for the rabble to rally at one point for any length of time, because several public schools will be involved, and the University of Georgia, at Athens, is already desegregated, and here in Atlanta, Georgia Tech, which the people also love, will be desegregated by that time. Where can the mob go?"

My friend was right: There were no mobs in Atlanta, or in Dallas, Galveston, Fort Lauderdale, Miami, Memphis, Little Rock, and New Orleans, all of them the scenes of new desegregation, or at the University of Georgia or at Georgia

Tech. Only the remote liberal who never felt a wound will disparage Atlanta's desegregation, and that of other Southern cities, as merely "token." The Negro students were few who found their way to formerly all-white schools, but in the minds of the extremists, it takes just one to desegregate. That several Negro pupils entered formerly all-white schools in, say, Atlanta, is a phenomenon that Southerners will know is almost beyond belief. They thought it couldn't happen there.

The final turning for the better in Georgia came, probably, when Governor Ernest Vandiver, having in effect returned Atlanta's schools to the people of Atlanta, said eventually, if belatedly, that he would use "whatever force is necessary" to keep down violence and disorder in Georgia. Atlanta, he said, must obey the federal court desegregation order "unless Georgia wants to secede from the United States and fire on Fort McPherson." Those mutterings you may have heard, at about that time, may have come from Governor Patterson, in Alabama, and Governor Orval Faubus, in Arkansas. They still don't like anybody who's soft on desegregation.

My traveling companion had returned to Chicago, but from Atlanta I flew to North Carolina. There I was informed almost immediately by a friend, "Segregation is dead. Now all we've got to do is bury it."

By this time I was prepared to believe him. I had come to believe, and still believe, that it's going to be a long, hard funeral, but funeral it will be, with many rejoicers and many mourners, and a few stubborn characters here and there who'll never admit that the old fellow is really dead. Three weeks before, when I left Chicago, I had not been prepared for this belief—for this change, or for other changes. Industrialization, the ease of travel, labor unions, the arrival of many new people

from other sections and the departure of many Southerners
for other places, the return of Army and Navy veterans who
have seen the world, the force of outside opinion, the knowledge that the suppression of a colored race makes poor propaganda for the South and for the nation in a world predominantly colored, the impact of television programs that bring
un-Southern voices and un-Southern ways into the very living
rooms of the Southerners (the unmistakably white Richie
Ashburn shakes hands with the unmistakably black Ernie
Banks when he completes a home run circuit, and all the nation sees)—these are the changes, they are preparing the way
for changes, they are themselves making changes.

Yet—I pondered in Chapel Hill, doing some research, talking to friends, walking the ancient campus—yet with all the
change, the old complexities live on, and the more the change,
the more obvious and even painful the complexities become.
They have, in these days, become perplexities that cause many
a Southerner to shake his head in fear and bewilderment.

Take segregation itself. On that Southern tour of mine I
did not, of course, talk to all Southerners, and perhaps not even
enough of them to impress Dr. Gallup. But I came away believing, for the first time, that most white Southerners, except
for the types that join the Klan and the White Citizens'
Councils, know that never again will the master-servant relationship of white and Negro be possible, that a new relationship is slowly establishing itself: a man-to-man, human-
being-to-human-being relationship that will eventually create
equality if not respect and affection.

Yet I left my Southern home believing that most white
Southerners still do not want this change. They like their
old ways—what they think of as the old, comfortable, unquestioned, unchallenged, unchallengeable "Southern way of life,"

by which they mean segregation in all its manifestations. And yet they are law-abiding citizens (again excepting the relatively few Kluxers, Council members, and the like). They do not advocate or desire violence. They would not themselves take up lead pipe or baseball bat and try to beat the brains out of a Negro or a Yankee or a newspaper reporter or photographer at a bus station. The people who did take up weapons against the Freedom Riders and innocent bystanders were, without a doubt, I think, the sort of rabble you'd find in any city (including my adopted home, Chicago, where, upon my return, I read that Negroes made homeless by a fire had been removed from a church refuge because a jeering crowd of whites gathered outside; and where I remembered mobs in South America, in Japan, in Africa, and slaughter in Russia and China, and told myself that no people, anywhere, stood alone in splendid virtue or in bloody idiocy).

In a number of differing ways, many Southerners said to me during my tour that nobody was proud of Alabama's performance at the bus stations. Some Alabamans had only contempt for the Birmingham police commissioner, Eugene (Bull) Connor, and their governor, John Patterson, a pair of rabid segregationists who created new notoriety for themselves, their state, the South and the nation as a result of the mob scenes. Nor, I believe, do most Southerners want to fight segregation by closing their schools. They love their schools —in many places they've supported them and educated their children at great sacrifice to themselves—and they know that education, in this world they live in now, is not a luxury but an imperative. As I had learned, the way for the desegregation of schools in Atlanta was cleared when the University of Georgia faced possible closing because two Negroes had enrolled there. The Georgia politicians simply called off massive resistance. The schools of Prince Edward County, Virginia, were still closed to avoid desegregation, but a visitor there recently was told by a local businessman, "I don't know anybody who's proud of what we've done." Perhaps most Southerners realize what a group of University of North Carolina researchers found in a study of Norfolk, Va., which closed its schools for a short time rather than accept desegregation. The study concludes:

> There is Little Rock and there is Norfolk. Tragedy is writ large in both cases. For any and all other cities, the conclusion is inevitable. There is no area of choice regarding whether eventually a community will have public schools. Only the process of reaching the decision offers a set of alternatives. Little Rock did without public schools before concluding that it couldn't do without public schools. Norfolk had to padlock its public schools before it realized that public schools couldn't be padlocked. Somewhere there are other cities facing or destined to face the decisions Norfolk and Little Rock faced.

I don't think that many more public schools will be closed during this funeral that we're discussing. Nor, I believe, will there be widespread violence as the rites continue. Southern businessmen, like businessmen everywhere, want more business, and closed schools and violence aren't likely to attract the industry they're all struggling to get for their states and communities. The leadership toward moderation and even widespread desegregation, then, may come not from the liberals but from the politicians, as in Georgia, or the businessmen, as in Birmingham. Dr. Rupert B. Vance, an authority on population and human geography at the University of North Carolina, said to me, "Industry won't move, or doesn't want to move, to places that don't have good schools. I understand that the business people in Virginia got after the politicians and said that massive resistance would ruin Virginia's chances to get industry. [Virginia, like Georgia, switched from massive resistance to local option.] Little Rock has been shunned by industry ever since that bad Faubus flareup."

And so, now, many Southerners find themselves in what must at times seem an insoluble dilemma. They don't want desegregation and are powerless to oppose it. It is coming in such a fashion that they can't oppose it in any way that will not penalize them, or make them ridiculous, or lead them into lawlessness and violence, or all three. In the resulting paralysis, desegregation is making its way toward completion, as it will continue to do, slowly, perhaps, but certainly and implacably.

This is a new complexity overlaid upon old complexities. For instance, the Negro in many sections of the South has long been denied the vote. For decades this un-American practice went unquestioned (or so it seemed to me, in the South of my growing up). Now it is becoming increasingly apparent, since the question has been raised, that you look at least silly if you go on rejecting the Negro Ph.D. at the polls while accepting the semiliterate white. And while I was in the South, *Gone with the Wind* was being shown in theaters everywhere and Confederate flags were flying in observance of the Civil War centennial. Yet most Southerners know now that the old South is a dream in the drugged brain of the nostalgic and the romantic; that only a minute fraction of the population really owned slaves and lived in mansions like Scarlett O'Hara's; and that anyway factories and office buildings stand now where it once stood, and massa raises not cotton but livestock and owns fleets of tractors and Cadillacs, and his faithful field hands have all moved North. The South has lived on its dreams; and the dreams have now become nightmares at bus stations.

You also have in the South a political relic of the old days that most of the Southern states are struggling with (as are other states too, of course). This is the domination of the legislatures by the rural counties. It results from the failure to reapportion, a failure that persists in defiance of all law and constitution. In Alabama, for instance, legislative representation is still based on the census of 1900, when the agricultural Black Belt counties were comparatively large in population and such industrial centers as Birmingham and Huntsville were comparatively small. The Black Belt has been steadily losing population, the others gaining by spectacular percentages; and yet the Alabama legislature still bears the old proportions among its members. A recent study that I found in Chapel Hill shows how widespread this imbalance is (and it is by no means confined to the South). In Camden County, small and rural, in eastern North Carolina, each legislator represents 5,440 persons; in industrial Guilford County 51,-105. In Georgia, rural Echols County has 2,964 persons for each representative; Fulton County (Atlanta) 130,692. It is the overrepresented rural areas that harbor and export the most violent of the racists, the newer industrial areas that are proceeding with desegregation. The cities want the legislatures reapportioned, but they know they're asking the rural politicians to vote themselves out of existence. Even with the help the Supreme Court gave the cities early in 1962, its going to be a long, hard struggle. The politician's first instinct is for survival.

The political nature of the South (and in the South politics is often not only a profession, it's a way of life) is further complicated by the dual nature of the electorate. In city, county, and state, the Democratic Party is always dominant; yet many of the new rich, and of the old rich and the in-between and the poor, vote Democratic locally but Republican in national elections often enough and strongly enough to carry their counties, and sometimes their states, for the Republican presidential candidate. For the new South that is emerging is, I believe, a conservative South. This is obvious enough, when you consider the votes of many Southerners in Congress and the acts of many Southern legislatures. To this natural conservatism (tempered at times by an old liberal tradition that harks back to the agrarians) has now been added the conservatism of a new middle class, much of it accounted for by the people brought in by new business and new industry.

And yet these conservative Southerners everywhere cling to the universal dogma that it's socialism if it helps the other fellow, but not if it helps you. No member of the National Association of Manufacturers, I dare say, has ever been so swayed by NAM propaganda that he has turned down a big federal contract. No congressman of my acquaintance has been brave or foolhardy enough to vote against a fat project for his state or district, and no local chamber of commerce has ever failed to applaud this federal largess, while both congressmen and the national chamber of commerce have continued on and on deploring the increase in federal spending and the spread of socialism. Just so in the South. In Huntsville, Alabama, there's a businessman named Dan Boone who was honored in 1961 with a second term as president of the Associated Tennessee Valley Chambers of Commerce. As the official announcement put it, he was re-elected because of "the splendid work that he has done in helping beat down anti-TVA policy in the U.S. Chamber of Commerce."

When the wall of the lock fell at Wheeler Dam, one of the TVA installations on the Tennessee River, transportation was stalled throughout the valley and businessmen everywhere were troubled; and the price of corn rose on the exchanges. If all the TVA power should fail suddenly, millions of men, women, and children would be engulfed in darkness, meat would spoil in thousands of refrigerators, and many an industry would tell its workers to go home and wait for a brighter day. You won't find much anti-TVA sentiment in the TVA area, whatever party it supports, and conservative Southern politicians who deplore federal interference in the South and preach states' rights for all are proud to join their names to the vast federal projects for their conservative constituents, who are delighted to get them. They profess to see no contradiction here, and perhaps there is none, but the whole thing does seem a bit complex.

For the returning Southerner, the whole South is complexity where once he knew simplicity. Desegregation, Freedom Riders, sit-ins, read-ins, wade-ins, court orders, white and black side by side on buses and in airport waiting rooms, massive resistance and piecemeal surrender—the old South is being attacked from all sides these days, from within almost as much as from without, and it is fighting back in despair and futility. The old Southerner is unprepared, whatever his beliefs, for the changes, for the contrasts, and the contradictions.

In Chapel Hill, which is the home of the oldest state university in the country, he learns that a Negro student would be editor of the University of North Carolina's law review during the coming year; and he is told that this is the highest honor that can be bestowed upon a law student there; and he is told also that a member of the university's medical school faculty heads the state's equivalent of the White Citizens' Council. And then he remembers that in another Southern state, in a city potentially violent, he has heard this story about the white and the black in the Deep South:

A group of white men and women made friends with a group of Negro men and women. They found that they liked each other and that they had similar interests: jazz, the theater, literature, art. They began visiting in each other's homes. The Negroes asked their white friends, some time ago, what it was really like in some of their city's most fashionable eating places. We'll show you, replied the whites. And so they put turbans on the heads of their Negro friends and took them to the restaurants. They spoke Spanish all evening, and nobody ever knew.

They laughed. Some people are beginning to laugh at the absurdities. The Negroes always laughed at them, and now, on occasion, their laughter is open and frank. On a Southern newsstand, from a Southern lady who said, "Hope you enjoy it, and come again," I bought a copy of *Harper's Magazine* containing an article called "The American Negro's New Comedy Act," by a Negro writer, Louis E. Lomax, who was born in Georgia. At one point he reports:

> And while in New Orleans segregationists were bringing public education to a lamentable halt because of the school integration issue, subdued laughter was pulsing throughout the Negro community. Fact of the matter is that New Orleans' schools have been integrated since the turn of the century. The white schools are peppered with light-skinned Negroes passing for white. They pass during the school day and then go home to social life among their Negro friends and relatives. Fear of detection caused them to join the white boycott of the integrated schools, and when segregationist Judge Leon Perez of nearby St. Bernard Parish threw open the doors of the community's all-white schools to accommodate the boycotters, the light-skinned Negroes were among the first to go over and register.

The traveler reading about "light-skinned Negroes" reflects that there's been one kind of desegregation in the South since the beginning, and in a reader's letter to the editor of the *Birmingham Post-Herald* he reads, "For our country and our civilization to survive, we must preserve the purity of the white race."

And he eats a dinner of catfish and hushpuppies in an air-conditioned restaurant and finds out later that the catfish came in a frozen package and he knows from the taste that the corn-meal in the hushpuppies is the same terrible, sweetened, machine-ground stuff he'd get in any Yankee restaurant or grocery store, and somehow as he leaves the South again there's a place in his perplexity and in his pondering for red roses and Redstone rockets, side by side.

In the South, the nation, the world, this is the time of the rose and the time of the rocket. Perhaps it always was.

INDEX

responsible for violence, 150
talk segregation, 179
Pontius Pilate, 111-113
population
and cropland, close interrelation of, 81
gain, Virginia, 1930-1960, 121
loss, Virginia, 1865-1935, 121
movement from South, 81-82
two fastest growing counties, U.S., 123
world, color balance, 11-12
poverty, genteel, of "best" families, 30
pressure, economic, White Citizens' Council, 94
Price, Leontyne, 42
pride, Southern, occasion for, 77-78
Prince of Carpetbaggers, 76
Professor, Mister, form of address, 35-36
progress, industrial, in South, 44
Progressive Farmer, The, 81
projects, federal, vs. states' rights, 199
Prince Edward County, 47, 50, 195
pulpwood, 53

race, white, purity of, 201
railroads, desegregated, 45
Reconstruction, dangers of, 42-43, 124
Reed, Stanley F., Justice, 63
Republican, elected Alabama, South Carolina, Texas, 57
resistance
massive, 82, 199
massive, abandoned by Virginia, 125

passive, of Negro, 151-152
resources, of South, 13, 53-55
responsibility for bringing change, 74-75
Revolution, Industrial, and South, 30
Richmond, 55, 81, 127
Rich's, 188, 189
rights, civil, basic, 25-26; *see also* voting
Road Home, The, 129
Roanoke, 127
Robert E. Lee, 76
Robert, Joseph C., 117
Roll Sweet Chariot, 157
Roosevelt, F. D., 122

St. Augustine, 102
Salvation on a String, 157
Saturday Evening Post, The, 14, 141
schools, 47-50, 58
section, poorest, of U.S., 84
sectionalism, pre-Civil War, and nationalism today, 160
Seeds of Southern Change: The Life of Will W. Alexander, 3
segregation, 7-9, 14, 23, 29-31, 33, 137-140, 143, 149, 152, 153, 154, 158, 171, 175, 176, 177-179, 192, 193, 194
substitute for slavery, 30-31
segregationist
avoidance of Negro eyes, 36
behavior outside South, 37
Sellers, Charles G., Jr., 5
Sherwood, Robert, 111
silence, myth of, 7-8
Simmons, William, 92